CHESS TACTICS

for Students

John A. Bain

Project Editor
Robert Mitchell

l-p

LEARNING PLUS, INC.
Corvallis, Oregon

Published by Learning Plus, Inc.
P.O. Box 1476, Corvallis, Oregon 97339
Manufactured in the United States of America.
International Standard Book Number: 0-9639614-0-3

13 12 11 10 9 8 7 6

Credits
_____

Editorial: Stacey Mitchell
Cover design: Craig Beverly and Gary La Pado
John Bain photo: R.P.M.

Please send questions and recommendations to:
John A. Bain
Learning Plus, Inc.
P.O. Box 1476
Corvallis, Oregon 97339

www.ChessForStudents.com

www.ChessPuzzles.com

Dedication

Chess Tactics for Students is dedicated to you students, parents, coaches, volunteers, tournament organizers, directors, and sponsors who make chess play and chess competition a great joy for us all. Your time and effort are very much appreciated.

Contents

To the Chess Coach

Chess Tactics for Students is an instructional workbook containing 434 carefully selected problems presented in a worksheet format. *Chess Tactics for Students* was extensively field tested with elementary, middle-school, and high-school students over a four-year period prior to its publication in 1993. Since that time, *Chess Tactics for Students* has become one of the best selling and most popular books ever written for beginning chess players.

A versatile design makes *Chess Tactics for Students* ideal for independent study and homework as well as for chess club and classroom instruction. The worksheet format enables self correction with minimal dependence on direct help from a chess coach, teacher, or parent.

Organizational Design

Each of the first thirteen chapters consists of 31 problems:

- an introductory page presenting the chapter tactic with a sample problem
- two instructional pages containing 4 problems with explanations of the correct move sequence(s) of each problem
- thirteen problem pages, each containing 2 problems, where problems are presented from the least difficult to the most difficult

The Answer Key

The Answer Key for *Chess Tactics for Students* is now bound-in the book. You, the chess teacher, will develop your own philosophy about how best to use the Answer Key with your students. Many coaches find that students learn best when they consult the Answer Key only *after* they've completed a number of assigned problems. We are all tempted to look up answers before we've given our best effort and early access to answers can interfere with good learning habits.

What is the best way to use this book?

The recommended way to use *Chess Tactics for Students* is as follows:

- Review the use of short algebraic notation on pages viii and ix.
- Assign the first 5 problems of each chapter as an overview to all 13 tactics.
- Use the Student Log on page 228 and to check each student's ability level.
- Have each student correct the problems they've done in the overview.
- After students have completed the overview, have them work through the book, chapter-by chapter.
- On a chapter-by-chapter basis, have students record their progress on the Student Log, provided on page 228.
- Encourage students to identify and practice newly-learned tactics in both instructional and recreational chess games.

To the Student

Welcome to *Chess Tactics for Students*. In this book, you will discover the secrets of grandmaster play—aggressive tactics that help turn beginners into experts. Players unfamiliar with these tactics will be at your mercy!

What is a tactic?

A tactic is a move (or sequence of moves) that gives you an immediate advantage over your opponent.

What advantage does a tactic give?

Depending on your opponent's position, a tactic can enable you to

- win a piece
- win the *exchange*—the trade of a Knight or Bishop for a Rook
- checkmate your opponent
- draw a game in which you are way behind in pieces or in position
- force your opponent to make a game-losing move

What is covered in this book?

Chess Tactics for Students covers thirteen major chess tactics, organized into chapters. Beginning chapters present the most frequently encountered and easily understood tactics. Later chapters present less frequently encountered and more difficult tactics. A concluding chapter of quizzes gives you a chance to review your skills.

What is the best way to use this book?

To begin, make sure you understand *short algebraic notation*. This notation is discussed on the next two pages. Short algebraic notation is used throughout *Chess Tactics for Students* and is the form in which you will record answers to problems.

For each problem, record the correct move sequence as indicated. If it is "White to move," pretend you are playing the White pieces and write White's correct moves and Black's responses on the blank lines provided. On some problems, you will write two possible lines of play. **Some moves and symbols are written on the lines for you.** Also, each problem has an accompanying **Hint** for help when you need it.

The first step in learning tactics is to work the first five problems in each chapter. Start with Chapter 1 and continue chapter-by-chapter through the book. This will give you an overview of all the major tactics and will help you start looking for them in your day-to-day chess games. After completing the first five problems in each chapter, go back and complete each chapter. At each step, check your answers in the **Answer Key** to make sure you are working carefully. A **Student Log** is provided on page 228 for you to record your progress.

Chess Notation

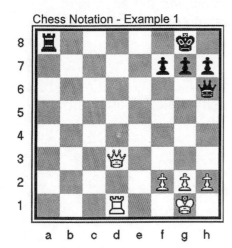

Chess Notation - Example 1

Chess Tactics for Students uses **short algebraic notation**, the notation endorsed by the United States Chess Federation and commonly used throughout the world today. Students should record their answers in this notation.

In short algebraic notation, each square on a chess board is identified by a letter followed by a number. The letter identifies a file (column), and the number identifies a rank (row). Each square is uniquely identified by its file letter and row number. Look at Example 1 at the left.

- The White King is on g1; the Black King is on g8.
- The White Queen is on d3; the Black Queen is on h6.
- The White Rook is on d1; the Black Rook is on a8.
- The White pawns are on f2, g2, and h2; the Black pawns are on f7, g7, and h7.

To identify a piece (except the Knight and the pawns), write the first letter of the name of the piece Write N to identify a Knight, and do not write any letter to identify a pawn. Capital letters identify pieces (K, Q, R, B, and N), while lower-case letters identify squares (b2, c5, etc.).

To record a move, write the letter of the piece followed by the name of the square to which the piece will move. Write Qd8+ to indicate a White Queen move to d8. "+" indicates "check."

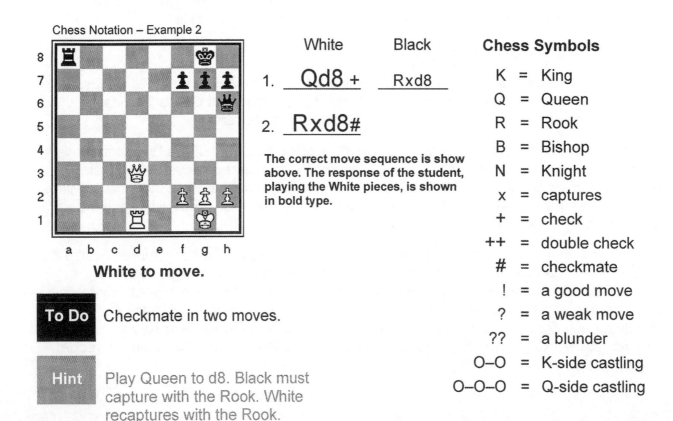

Chess Notation – Example 2

White to move.

	White	Black
1.	Qd8 +	Rxd8
2.	Rxd8#	

The correct move sequence is show above. The response of the student, playing the White pieces, is shown in bold type.

Chess Symbols

K	=	King
Q	=	Queen
R	=	Rook
B	=	Bishop
N	=	Knight
x	=	captures
+	=	check
++	=	double check
#	=	checkmate
!	=	a good move
?	=	a weak move
??	=	a blunder
O–O	=	K-side castling
O–O–O	=	Q-side castling

To Do Checkmate in two moves.

Hint Play Queen to d8. Black must capture with the Rook. White recaptures with the Rook.

Chess Notation

Chess Notation - Example 3

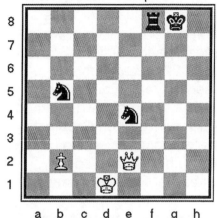

Black to move.

	White	Black
1.	• • •	Nec3+
2.	bxc3	Nxc3+
3.	K moves	Nxe2

The student, playing the Black pieces, chose to move the Knight on the "e" file to c3 as Black's first move.

To Do Win the White Queen in three moves.

Hint Use a Knight sacrifice check. Then, use a Knight Fork check.

When you can move more than one piece of the same kind to the same square, you must identify the piece that is to be moved. To do this, follow the symbol of the piece with its file letter.

In Example 3 at the left, you can move either Black Knight to c3.

- To move the Knight on the "b" file, write . . . Nbc3.
- To move the Knight on the "e" file, write . . . Nec3.

In positions where both pieces are on the same file, follow the symbol of the piece with its rank number instead of its file number.

Chess Notation – Example 4

White to move.

To Do Avoid a stalemate draw. Come out a Rook ahead.

Hint Promote the pawn to a piece other than a Queen.

	White	Black
1.	c8 = R	

	White	Black
1.	c8 = Q ??	
	stalemate	

In short algebraic notation, you record a pawn move simply by identifying the square to which the pawn moves. In Example 4, write "c8" to indicate moving the White pawn from c7 to c8.

To record a pawn promotion (reaching the 8th rank), follow the square notation with an equals sign (=) and the letter of the piece the player chooses.

In Example 4, White promotes the c7 pawn to a Rook (c8 = R). White realizes it would be a blunder (??) to promote to a Queen (c8 = Q??), a promotion that results in a stalemate draw.

Interesting Chess Facts

- Who is the greatest chess player of all time? Of living players, most Grandmasters would likely say Bobby Fischer, Garry Kasparov, or Anatoly Karpov—each of whom has won the world championship and held in for an extended period of time. Some would mention Judit Polgar who, at fifteen years of age in 1992, became the youngest Grandmaster in the history of chess. Of deceased players, a good choice is Paul Morphy, an American player from New Orleans. In 1964, Morphy was named by future World Champion Fischer as number one on his list of "The Ten Greatest Masters in History." Morphy (1837–1884) gave up chess at the age of 24, and began a legal career that unfortunately never prospered. He then withdrew from society, thinking that life as a chess professional was not a proper career for a gentleman!

- Bored with standard openings, a group of British players organized a tournament in London during 1868 in which the starting positions of the knights and bishops were reversed. The tournament was played with a great deal of interest and enthusiasm, but the idea did not remain popular very long!

- The shortest championship chess game on record lasted one move! In the final round of the Palma Interzonal Tournament held in 1970, Oscar Panno showed up for his game with Bobby Fischer but resigned after Fischer, playing white, made his first move. By resigning, Panno lost but avoided forfeiting the game, allowing Fischer to pick up valuable tournament points with the win. If Panno had forfeited the game by not showing up at all, Fischer would not have received tournament points.

- The longest official chess game took 193 moves to complete, lasted 24 hours 30 minutes, and was played over six sittings. The game was between Stepak and Maschian in the semifinals of the Israeli Championship of 1980. Maschian played a Queen's Indian Defense, but Stepak, playing white, won the exhausting battle.

- The most misunderstood rule in chess is the *three-time repetition rule*. While many players think that a series of moves must be repeated three times before a draw can be declared, it is actually the position that must be repeated three times. What many players do not realize is that the same position can occur three times—each time separated by perhaps a dozen moves—and still be a draw when claimed!

- Do you ever wonder how many different opening variations are possible in a chess game? Approximately 9,000,000 different variations are possible after only the first three moves by each player.

- Do you ever wonder how most tournament chess games usually end? Ernest Rubin, an American statistician did an analysis of 1,005 major tournament games and found the following results: 35% of games end in draws (11% by perpetual check), 62% end in resignation; 2% end in checkmate; and fewer than 1% end by a player running out of time.

Interesting Chess Quotes

- **Chess, like love, like music, has the power to make us happy.**
  Dr. Siegbert Tarrasch (1862–1934), German Chess Grandmaster and teacher.

- **Chess is not merely an idle amusement . . . life is a kind of chess.**
  Benjamin Franklin (1706–1790), American statesman, writer, scientist, and inventor.

- **There is no other game so esteemed, so profound and venerable as chess; in the realm of play, chess stands alone in dignity.**
  Ely Culbertson (1891–1955), Romanian-born American Bridge Champion.

- **Chess is a fine entertainment.**
  Leo Tolstoy (1828–1910), Russian novelist and social critic.

- **Chess is a game that reflects most honor on human wit.**
  Francois Voltaire (1694–1764), French philosopher, dramatist, and essayist.

- **The game of chess is the touchstone of the intellect.**
  Yohann von Goethe (1749–1832), German poet, dramatist, novelist, and philosopher.

- **It is hopeless to try to make a machine that plays perfect chess.**
  Norbert Weiner (1894–1964), American mathematician, inventor of cybernetics.

- **Chess is an international language.**
  Emmanuel Lasker (1868–1950), German World Chess Champion, 1894–1921.

- **Chess is . . . the same sort of art as painting and sculpture.**
  Jose Capablanca (1888–1942), Cuban World Chess Champion, 1921–1927.

- **Thank you, darling, for learning to play chess. It is an absolute necessity in any well-organized family.**
  Alexander Puskin (1799–1838), Russian poet and author (speaking to his wife).

- **When in doubt, take a pawn!**
  Wilhelm Steinitz (1835–1900), Austrian World Chess Champion, 1866–1894.

- **The mistakes are all there waiting to be made!**
  Dr. Savielly Tartakover (1899–1956), Russian-born French chess player and writer.

- **Chess is a sea in which a gnat may drink and an elephant may bathe.**
  Old Russian proverb.

Chess in History

From "The Three Ages of Man," a manuscript of the 15th century, depicting chess in the castle of King Louis XI of France.

The author of the manuscript is believed to be Estienne Porchier.

"The Game of Chess"

A 16th century engraving by G. B. Leonetti, based on a work by Anguiscola.

The Power of Tactics

Chess is 99% tactics.

Richard Teichmann

Chess, a contest between two opponents pushing 32 odd-shaped pieces around a 64-square board, captivates the minds and hearts of people all over the world as it has for centuries. Great players have left their ideas, descriptions, and even their names on favorite attacks and defenses: Ruy Lopez, Bird's Defense, Max Lange Attack, Fischer Variations, Hedgehog Defense, Fried Liver Attack, Orangutan—just to name a few.

Talk to a grandmaster and you'll learn of a favorite opening, a brilliant middle game strategy, or a famous ending. You'll hear of victories that followed long struggles where one strategy proved stronger than another. But the most enjoyable stories are those that involve a **tactic**—a surprise move that is so powerful that the opponent's position crumbled and victory quickly followed.

Tactics often do not involve long term strategy. A tactic is often a quick trick, a card up a grandmaster's sleeve waiting to be played. Like all tricks, though, tactics can be learned by anyone. Whether you are a grandmaster or a beginner (a *duffer*, *patzer*, or *fish* in chess talk), you can learn to use tactics to surprise and defeat unwary opponents.

To learn tactics you must see and practice them. In the pages ahead, you will learn to recognize, set up, and use 13 winning chess tactics. As your first step, do five problems in each chapter. Then, work all of the problems in each chapter. Write your answers on the lines provided—but only after you are confident you are correct. The quizzes in Chapter 14 give you a chance to review and strengthen your skills.

To get the most from your study:

- Know the board. Be sure you can use algebraic notation to name squares and to write moves.

- Use the hints to your advantage. First, try to find the best move without reading the hint. Do each problem in your head or on a board. Then, use the hint as your guide. Remember, no one becomes an expert on tactics without first seeing them in action.

- When you feel comfortable with a tactic, *talk tactics* to a friend. Name the tactic and use chess pieces to show your friend how it works.

- Look for tactics in your own chess games and share them with your team or class. Make each tactic part of your chess arsenal.

- Above all, enjoy your study and have fun playing chess.

1 PINS introduction

A **pin** holds a piece in place so that it cannot move without losing something of greater value or putting its King in check. Some pins are simple, such as the Rook Pin shown in Diagram 1. Other pins take two or more moves to set up.

Diagram 1

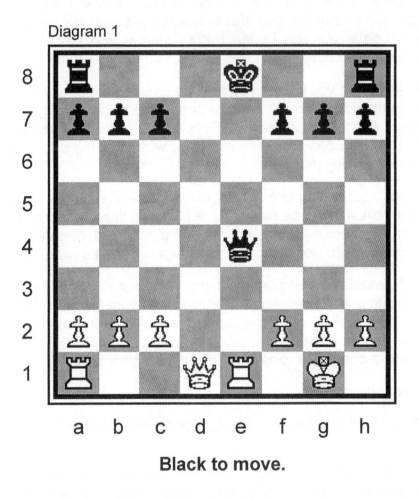

Black to move.

White just played the Rook to e1, *pinning* the Black Queen to its King. Whatever Black does, White will capture the Black Queen on the next move.

Circle the Black piece that is pinned by the White Rook.

1 Pins instruction

Diagram 2

White to move.

White	Black		White	Black
1. Re1	Qxe1 +		1. Re1	0–0 ??
2. Qxe1+			2. Rxe4	

This one is done for you.

 To Do Win the Black Queen for a Rook in two moves.

How Use a Rook Pin. Play Re1, pinning the Black Queen to the King on the e file. On the next move, White will win the Black Queen.

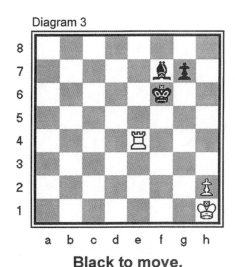

Diagram 3

Black to move.

White	Black		White	Black
1. • • •			1. • • •	
2. K moves			2. P Moves	+

Your turn now!

 To Do Win the White Rook in two moves.

How Use a Bishop Pin. Play Bd5, pinning the White Rook on e4. Black's next move is Bxe4, winning the Rook.

3

1 PINS instruction

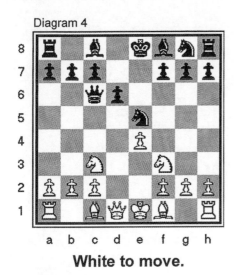

Diagram 4

8 7 6 5 4 3 2 1
a b c d e f g h

White to move.

	White	Black		White	Black
1.	_____	Q x b5	1.	_____	Bd7
2.	_____		2.	_____	

To Do Win the Black Queen for a Bishop in two moves.

How Use a Bishop Pin. Play Bb5, pinning the Black Queen to the King. On the next move, White will capture the Black Queen.

Diagram 5

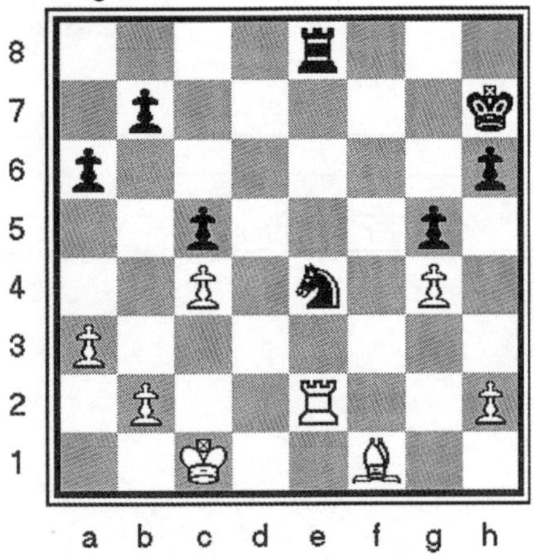

8 7 6 5 4 3 2 1
a b c d e f g h

White to move.

	White	Black
1.	_____	Rxe4
2.	_____	Any Move
3.	_____	

To Do Win the Black Knight in three moves.

How Play Rxe4. If Black plays Rxe4, use a Bishop Pin by playing Bd3, pinning the Black Rook to its King. White can then capture the Black Rook on the next move.

4

1 Pins

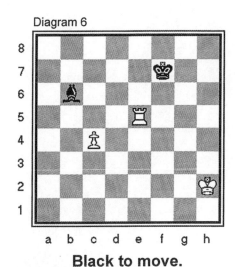

Diagram 6

Black to move.

	White	Black		White	Black
1.	• • •	_____	1.	• • •	_____
2.	K moves	_____	2.	P moves	____ +

To Do Win the White Rook in two moves.

Hint Use a Bishop Pin.

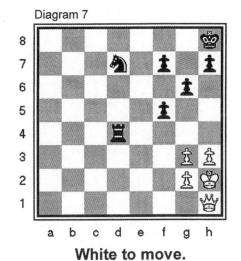

Diagram 7

White to move.

	White	Black
1.	_____	Any move
2.	_____	

To Do Win the Black Rook in two moves.

Hint Use a Queen Pin.

1 Pins

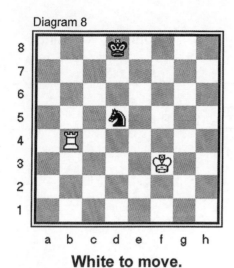

Diagram 8

White	Black
1. _____	K moves
2. _____	

White to move.

To Do Win the Black Knight in two moves.

Hint Use a Rook Pin.

Diagram 9

White	Black
1. _____	Bd7
2. _____	

White to move.

To Do Win the Black Knight on c6 for a pawn in two moves.

Hint Use a Bishop Pin and a pawn attack.

6

1 Pins

Diagram 10

Black to move.

	White	Black
1.	• • •	_____
2.	Bd2	_____

To Do Win the White Queen for a Bishop in two moves.

Hint Use a Bishop Pin.

Diagram 11

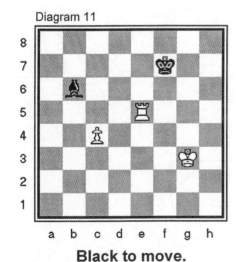

Black to move.

	White	Black		White	Black
1.	• • •	_____	1.	• • •	_____
2.	Kf4	_____	2.	Kf4	_____
3.	P moves	_____ +	3.	K moves	_____

To Do Win the White Rook in three moves.

Hint Use a Bishop Pin, followed by an attack on the pinned piece by the King.

1 Pins

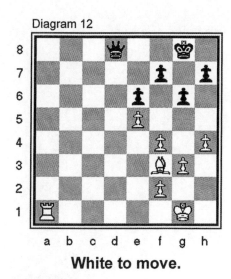

Diagram 12

White to move.

White	Black	White	Black
1. _____	Qxa8	1. _____	Qf8
2. _____		2. _____ +	

To Do Win the Black Queen for a Rook in two moves.

Hint Use a Rook Pin.

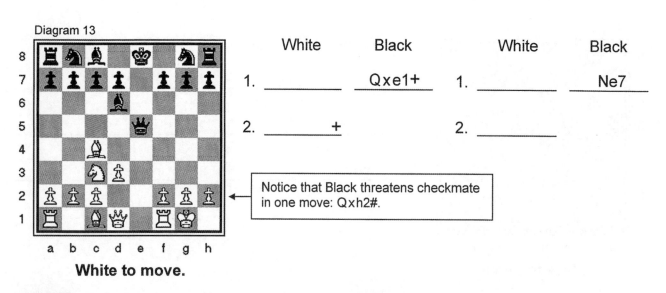

Diagram 13

White to move.

White	Black	White	Black
1. _____	Qxe1+	1. _____	Ne7
2. _____ +		2. _____	

Notice that Black threatens checkmate in one move: Qxh2#.

To Do Win the Black Queen for a Rook in two moves.

Hint Use a Rook Pin.

1 Pins

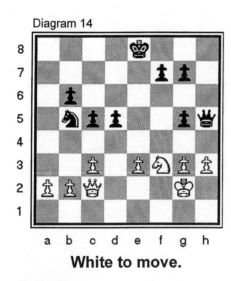

Diagram 14

White to move.

	White	Black		White	Black
1.		Ke7	1.		g4
2.			2.	+	K moves
			3.		

To Do Win the Black Knight in two or three moves.

Hint Use a Queen Pin.

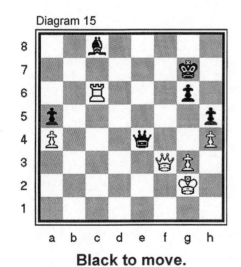

Diagram 15

Black to move.

	White	Black
1.	• • •	+
2.		
3.	Any move	

To Do Win the White Rook in three moves.

Hint Use a Queen trade, followed by a Bishop Pin!

1 Pins

Diagram 16

	White	Black
1.	_____	a6
2.	_____	Any move
3.	_____	

White to move.

To Do Win the Black Rook in three moves.

Hint Use a Queen Pin, followed by a pawn attack.

Diagram 17

	White	Black
1.	N x d5	Q x d5??
2.	_____	Q x c4
3.	_____	

White to move.

To Do Win the d5 pawn and the Black Queen for a Knight and Bishop—if Black plays . . . Q x d5??

Hint Use a Knight sacrifice, followed by a Bishop Pin.

Diagram 18

White to move.

	White	Black		White	Black
1.	_____	cxb4	1.	_____	Any other
2.	_____		2.	Nd3!	

To Do Win a pawn on b4 in two moves.

Hint Use a temporary Knight sacrifice on b4. The Knight offer is possible because the pawn on c5 is pinned,

---

Diagram 19

White to move.

	White	Black		White	Black
1.	_____	Qxe5?	1.	_____	O–O!
2.	_____	Qxe1?	2.	d4!	
3.	_____ +				

To Do Win the Black Queen and a pawn for a Knight and Rook in three moves, or win the pawn on e5 in one move.

Hint Use a Knight sacrifice on e5, followed by a Rook Pin.

11

1 Pins

Diagram 20

White to move.

	White	Black
1.	_____	a6 !
2.	_____ +	_____
3.	_____	

To Do Win a Knight on c6 in three moves.

Hint Use a Bishop Pin and a Pawn attack.

Diagram 21

White to move.

	White	Black
1.	_____	Kg7
2.	_____	Any move
3.	_____	

To Do Win the Black Knight in three moves.

Hint Attack the pinned Knight two more times. Begin with Qh4!.

12

1 Pins

Diagram 22

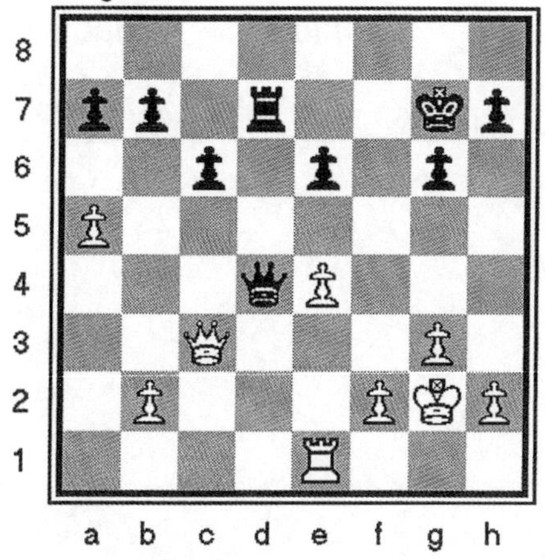

White to move.

	White	Black		White	Black
1.	_____	e5	1.	_____	Qxc3?
2.	_____		2.	_____ +	K moves
			3.	_____	

To Do Win the Black Queen for a Rook in two moves—or win the Black Rook in three moves if . . . Qxc3?

Hint Attack the pinned Black Queen with the White Rook.

Remember: Attack pinned pieces.

Diagram 23

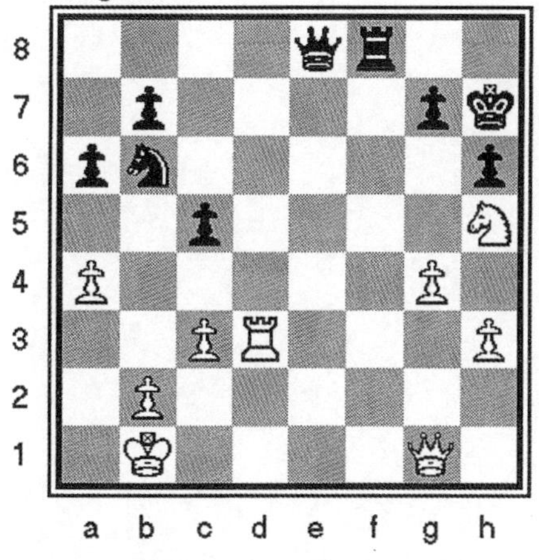

Black to move.

	White	Black
1.	• • •	_____
2.	Kc2	_____
3.	Any move	_____

To Do Win the White Rook for a pawn in three moves.

Hint Use a Queen Pin, followed by a pawn attack against the White Rook. (. . .Qe4 does not work because it allows White to play Qe3.)

13

Diagram 24

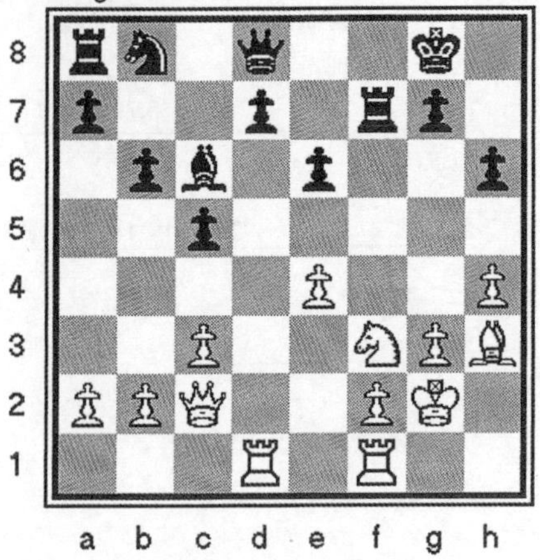

	White	Black		White	Black
1.	_____	Qf6	1.	_____	d×e6??
2.	_____ +		2.	_____ +	

White to move.

To Do Win a pawn and the Black Rook on f7 for a Bishop in two moves, or win a pawn and the Black Queen for a Bishop in two moves.

Hint Use a Bishop sacrifice, pinning the Black Rook to its King— followed by capturing the Rook or the Queen (if Black plays . . . d×e6??).

Diagram 25

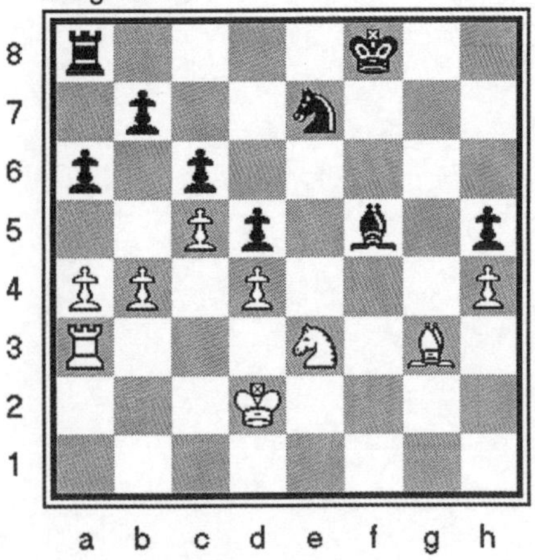

	White	Black
1.	_____	N×f5?
2.	_____	Any move
3.	_____	

White to move.

To Do Win a Black Knight on f5 in three moves.

Hint Capture the Bishop on f5, followed by a Rook Pin.

Diagram 26

White to move.

	White	Black		White	Black
1.	_____	Qxe4??	1.	_____	Qxe4??
2.	_____	Qxe1+	2.	_____	Nf6?
3.	_____+		3.	_____+	

To Do Win the Black Queen for a Rook and a pawn in three moves—if Black's first move is . . . Qxe4??

Hint White's first move guards the pawns on g2 and e4, by threat of a Rook Pin. Black blunders and captures the e4 pawn!

Diagram 27

Black to move.

	White	Black
1.	• • •	_____
2.	_____	_____
3.	Qxb7	_____

To Do Win the White Rook for a Bishop in three moves.

Hint Use a Queen sacrifice, followed by a Bishop Pin, winning back the Queen.

1 Pins

Diagram 28

8 7 6 5 4 3 2 1

a b c d e f g h

White to move.

White		Black
1. _____	+	Kg7/Kg8
2. _____	+	Kh8
3. _____	#	

The slash (/) is used to show that either of two moves is possible.

To Do Checkmate in three moves.

Hint Use a Queen check—possible because Black's g-pawn is pinned. Then, capture the g-pawn with check, followed by mate from the Queen.

Diagram 29

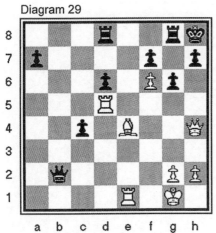

8 7 6 5 4 3 2 1

a b c d e f g h

White to move.

White		Black
1. _____	+	Kxh7
2. _____	#	

To Do Checkmate in two moves.

Hint Use a Queen sacrifice check, followed by a Rook checkmate. Mate is possible because Black's g-pawn is pinned.

16

1 Pins

Diagram 30

White to move.

	White	Black
1.	_____ +	Kxd8
2.	_____	

To Do Win the Black Queen for a Rook in two moves.

Hint Use a Rook sacrifice check (Rd8+). Then, capture the Black Queen. Winning the Queen is possible because the Black Knight is pinned.

Diagram 31

White to move.

	White	Black		White	Black
1.	_____	Nxc4	1.	_____	Ne7
2.	_____		2.	_____	Nbc8
			3.	_____	

To Do Win a Knight or Bishop on the "d" file for a pawn in two or three moves.

Hint Use a pawn attack and Rook Pin.

2 Back Rank Combinations introduction

A **Back Rank Combination** is based on the enemy King being fenced in by its own pawns and the fact that the back rank is not protected by a Rook or Queen. Some back rank combinations are simple, as shown in Diagram 32. Others take two or more moves to set up.

Diagram 32

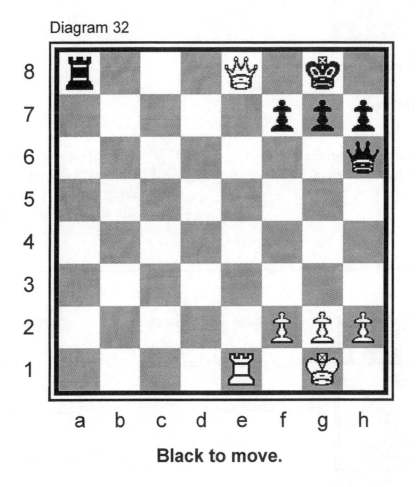

Black to move.

Black is in check by the White Queen, and the Black King is fenced in by its own pawns. Black's only legal move is Rook takes Queen (. . . Rxe8). Then, White plays Rook takes Rook, resulting in checkmate (Rxe8#).

Circle the White piece that checkmates the Black King.

18

2 Back Rank Combinations instruction

Diagram 33

White to move.

	White	Black
1.	Qd8 +	Rxd8
2.	Rxd8#	

This one is done for you.

 To Do Checkmate in two moves.

 How Use a Queen sacrifice check by playing Qd8+. Black's King is fenced in by its own pawns. Black's only legal move is . . . Rxd8. White then plays Rxd8#.

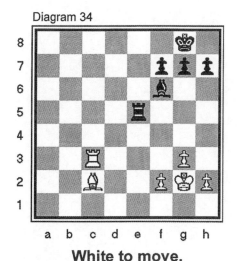

Diagram 34

White to move.

	White	Black
1.	_____ +	Bd8
2.	_____ +	Re8
3.	_____ #	

Your turn now!

 To Do Checkmate in three moves.

 How White plays Rc8+. Black can block (interpose) the check two times: . . . Bd8 and . . . Re8. Finally, Black will be mated as White captures each piece.

19

2 Back Rank Combinations instruction

Diagram 35

White to move.

	White		Black
1.		+	
2.			
3.		#	

 To Do Checkmate in three moves.

How White plays Qf8+. Black is forced to play . . . Rxf8. White recaptures with the f2 Rook. Black recaptures with the Queen. Black then mates by recapturing with the f1 Rook.

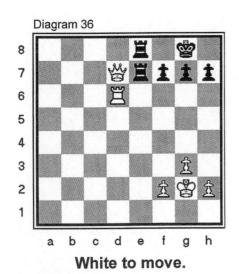

Diagram 36

White to move.

	White		Black
1.			Rxe7??
2.		+	
3.		#	

To Do Checkmate in three moves.

How White plays Qxe7!. If Black plays . . . Rxe7, then White plays Rd8+. Black can block the check with . . . Re8, but then White plays Rxe8#.

20

2 Back Rank Combinations

Diagram 37

Black to move.

White	Black
1. • • •	#

To Do Checkmate in one move.

Hint Use a Back Rank mate.

Diagram 38

White to move.

White	Black
1. #	

To Do Checkmate in one move.

Hint Use a Back Rank mate.

2 Back Rank Combinations

Diagram 39

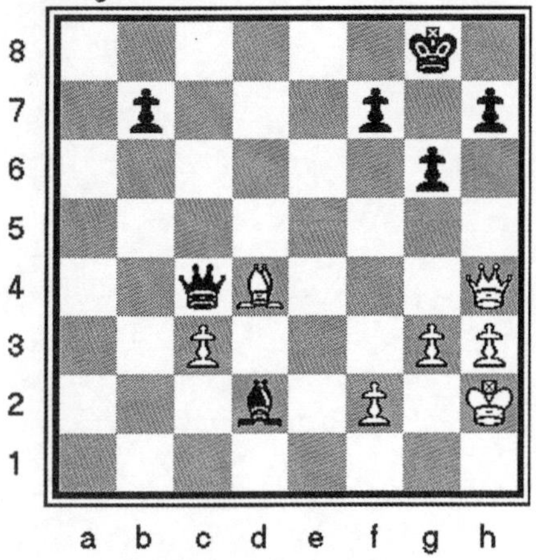

White to move.

White	Black
1. _____ #	

To Do Checkmate in one move.

Hint Use a Back Rank mate.

Diagram 40

White to move.

White	Black
1. _____ + _____	
2. _____ #	

To Do Checkmate in two moves.

Hint Use a Back Rank Combination, beginning with a Queen sacrifice.

2 Back Rank Combinations

Diagram 41

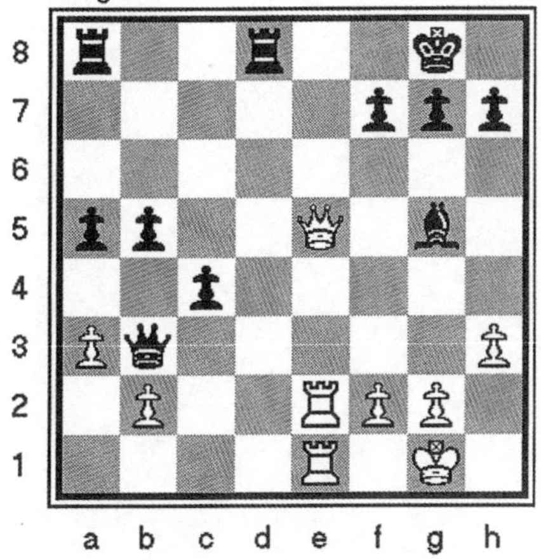

White to move.

	White	Black
1.	_____ +	_____
2.	_____ +	_____
3.	_____ #	

To Do Checkmate in three moves.

Hint Use a Back Rank Combination, beginning with a Queen sacrifice.

Diagram 42

White to move.

	White	Black
1.	_____ +	_____
2.	_____ +	_____
3.	_____ #	

To Do Checkmate in three moves.

Hint Use a Back Rank Combination. Notice that the White Queen is also attacking the f8 square.

23

2 Back Rank Combinations

Diagram 43

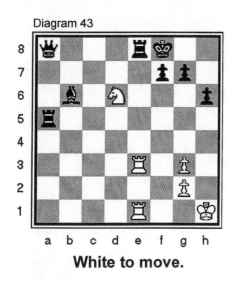

White to move.

White	Black
1. _____ +	_____
2. _____ #	

To Do   Checkmate in two moves.

Hint   Use a Back Rank Combination.

Diagram 44

White to move.

White	Black
1. _____ +	_____
2. _____ #	

To Do   Checkmate in two moves.

Hint   Use a Back Rank Combination. Notice that the White Bishop attacks Black's h7 flight square.

2 Back Rank Combinations

Diagram 45

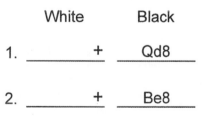

	White	Black
1.	_____ +	_____
2.	_____ +	_____
3.	_____ #	

White to move.

To Do Checkmate in three moves.

Hint Use a Back Rank Combination. Notice that the White Knight attacks Black's f7 flight square.

Diagram 46

	White	Black
1.	_____ +	Qd8
2.	_____ +	Be8
3.	_____ #	

White to move.

To Do Checkmate in three moves.

Hint Use a Back Rank Combination. Notice that the White Bishop attacks Black's h7 flight square.

25

2 Back Rank Combinations

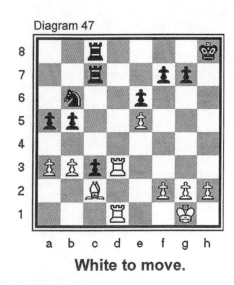

Diagram 47

White to move.

	White	Black
1.	_____ +	_____
2.	_____ #	

To Do Checkmate in two moves.

Hint Use a Back Rank Combination. Notice that the White Bishop attacks Black's h7 flight square after the White Rook moves away from d3.

Diagram 48

White to move.

	White	Black
1.	_____ +	Nxc8
2.	_____ +	Rd8
3.	_____ #	

To Do Checkmate in three moves.

Hint Use a Back Rank Combination. Notice that the White pawn on g6 attacks Black's f7 and h7 flight squares.

26

2 Back Rank Combinations

Diagram 49

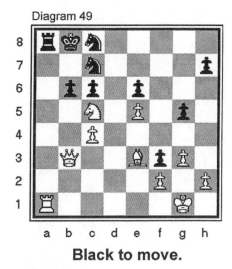

Black to move.

	White	Black
1.	• • •	+
2.	Bc1	+
3.	Qd1	#

To Do Checkmate in three moves.

Hint Use a Back Rank Combination. White can interpose (block the Rook check) two times, but cannot stop the checkmate.

Diagram 50

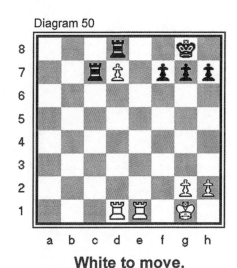

White to move.

	White	Black
1.	_____ +	_____
2.	_____ #	

To Do Checkmate in two moves.

Hint Use a Back Rank Combination that leads to a pawn promotion and checkmate.

27

2 Back Rank Combinations

Diagram 51

White to move.

	White	Black
1.	_____ +	_____
2.	_____ #	

To Do Checkmate in two moves.

Hint Use a Back Rank Combination that leads to a pawn promotion and checkmate.

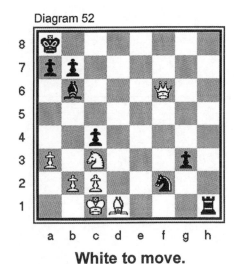

Diagram 52

White to move.

	White	Black
1.	_____ +	_____
2.	_____ #	

To Do Checkmate in two moves.

Hint Use a Back Rank Combination. Careful! The White Queen can check from three squares, but only one leads to checkmate.

2 Back Rank Combinations

Diagram 53

White to move.

	White	Black
1.	_____ +	_____
2.	_____ #	

To Do Checkmate in two moves.

Hint Use a Bank Rank Combination. Notice that the Black Bishop protects the e8 square.

Diagram 54

White to move.

	White	Black
1.	_____ +	Qc8
2.	_____ +	Ne8
3.	_____ #	

To Do Checkmate in three moves.

Hint Use a Bank Rank Combination. Notice that Black can interpose (block) two times after White's first check.

29

2 Back Rank Combinations

Diagram 55

Black to move.

	White	Black
1.	• • •	+
2.		#

To Do Checkmate in two moves.

Hint Use a Back Rank Combination beginning with a Bishop check.

Diagram 56

White to move.

	White	Black
1.	+	
2.	+	
3.	#	

To Do Checkmate in three moves.

Hint Use a Back Rank Combination.

2 Back Rank Combinations

Diagram 57

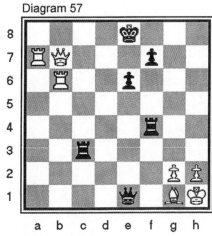

Black to move.

	White	Black
1.	• • •	_____ +
2.	_____	_____ #

To Do Checkmate in two moves.

Hint Use a Back Rank Combination, beginning with a Queen sacrifice check.

Diagram 58

White to move.

	White	Black
1.	_____ +	_____
2.	_____ #	

To Do Checkmate in two moves.

Hint Use a Back Rank Combination, beginning with a Queen sacrifice check.

31

2 Back Rank Combinations

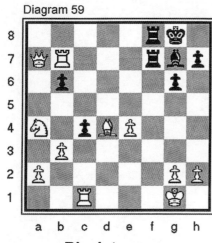

Diagram 59

Black to move.

	White	Black
1.	• • •	_____ +
2.	_____	_____ +
3.	_____	_____ #

To Do Checkmate in three moves.

Hint Use a Bishop check, followed by a Back Rank Combination that ends with a Rook checkmate.

Diagram 60

Black to move.

	White	Black
1.	• • •	_____ +
2.	Bxd4	_____ +
3.	_____	_____ +
4.	_____	_____ #

To Do Checkmate in four moves.

Hint Use a Queen sacrifice check, followed by a Bishop check. Follow that with a Back Rank Combination that ends with a Rook checkmate.

2 Back Rank Combinations

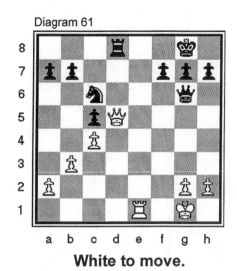

Diagram 61

White to move.

	White	Black
1.	_____ +	_____
2.	_____ #	

To Do Checkmate in two moves.

Hint Use a Back Rank Combination, beginning with a Queen sacrifice check.

Diagram 62

White to move.

	White	Black
1.	_____ +	_____
2.	_____ +	_____
3.	_____ #	

To Do Checkmate in three moves.

Hint Use a Back Rank Combination, beginning with a Rook check. Then, use a Queen sacrifice check, followed by a Rook checkmate.

33

3 Knight Forks introduction

A **Knight Fork** is a Knight (N) attack on two or more enemy pieces at the same time. Some Knight Forks are simple, as shown in Diagram 63. Others take two or more moves to set up.

Diagram 63

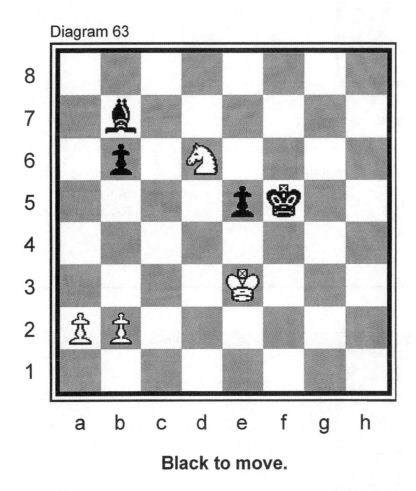

Black to move.

The White Knight is attacking the Black King and Bishop at the same time—forking them! Black must move the King, and then the Knight can capture the Black Bishop.

Circle the White piece that is forking the Black pieces.

34

3 Knight Forks instruction

Diagram 64

White to move.

White	Black
1. Nd6 +	K moves
2. Nxb7	

This one is done for you.

To Do Win the Black Bishop in two moves.

How White plays Nd6+, forking the Black King and Bishop. Black must move the King. Then, the White Knight captures the Black Bishop (Nxb7).

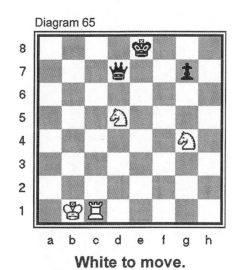

Diagram 65

White to move.

White	Black
1. _____ +	_____
2. _____ +	K moves
3. _____	

Your turn now!

To Do Win the Black Queen in three moves.

How White plays Ngf6+, forking the Black King and Queen. Black captures the Knight. Then, White recaptures with the other Knight (Ndxf6+), again forking the King and Queen.

3 Knight Forks instruction

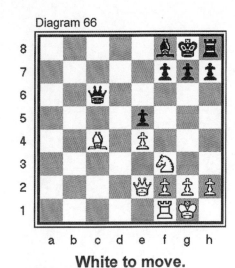

Diagram 66

White to move.

	White	Black
1.	_____ +	_____
2.	_____ +	K moves
3.	_____	

To Do Win the Black Queen and two pawns for a Bishop in three moves.

How White plays Bxf7+, sacrificing a Bishop and forcing Black to play . . . Kxf7. Then, White forks Black's King and Queen (Nxe5+), winning the Queen.

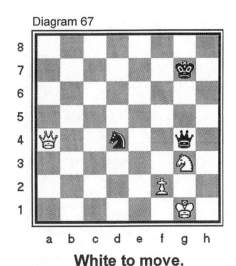

Diagram 67

White to move.

	White	Black
1.	_____ +	_____
2.	_____ +	K moves
3.	_____	

To Do Win the Black Knight in three moves.

How White plays Qxd4+, attacking the Black King and Queen. To save the Queen, Black plays . . . Qxd4. White then forks Black's King and Queen (Nf5+), winning the Black Queen.

36

3 Knight Forks

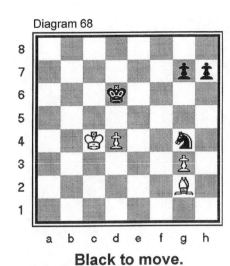

Diagram 68

Black to move.

	White	Black
1.	• • •	_____ +
2.	K moves	_____

To Do Win the White Bishop in two moves.

Hint Use a Knight Fork.

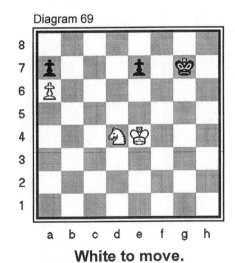

Diagram 69

White to move.

	White	Black
1.	_____	Kf6
2.	_____	

To Do Win a pawn in two moves.

Hint Use a Knight Fork.

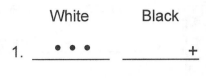

37

Diagram 70

White to move.

	White		Black
1.	_____	+	K moves
2.	_____		

To Do Win the Black pawn on d5 in two moves.

Hint Use a Knight Fork.

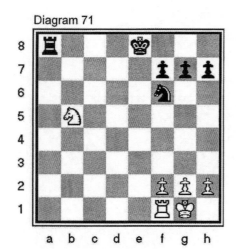

Diagram 71

White to move.

	White		Black
1.	_____	+	K moves
2.	_____		

To Do Win the Black Rook in two moves.

Hint Use a Knight Fork.

3 Knight Forks

Diagram 72

	White	Black
1.	_____ +	K moves
2.	_____	

White to move.

To Do Win the Black Queen for a Knight in two moves.

Hint Use a Knight Fork.

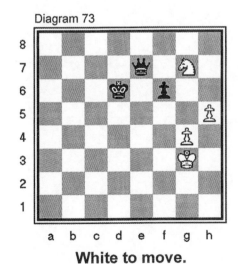

Diagram 73

	White	Black
1.	_____ +	K moves
2.	_____	

White to move.

To Do Win the Black Queen for a Knight in two moves.

Hint Use a Knight Fork.

3 Knight Forks

Diagram 74

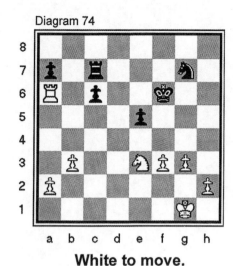

8   7   6   5   4   3   2   1

a   b   c   d   e   f   g   h

White to move.

White	Black
1. _____ +	K moves
2. _____	

To Do   Win the Black Rook in two moves.

Hint   Use a Knight Fork check. Notice that the Black pawn on c6 is pinned to its King and cannot move!

Diagram 75

8   7   6   5   4   3   2   1

a   b   c   d   e   f   g   h

Black to move.

White	Black
1. • • • _____	_____ +
2. K moves	_____

To Do   Win the White Queen in two moves.

Hint   Use a Knight Fork. Notice that the White Rook is pinned to its King and cannot move!

3 Knight Forks

Diagram 76

White to move.

	White	Black		White	Black
1.	_____ +	K moves	1.	_____ +	Bxd6??
2.	_____		2.	_____	

To Do Win the Black Bishop on b7 (or the Black Queen) in two moves.

Hint Use a Knight Fork and Bishop pin.

Diagram 77

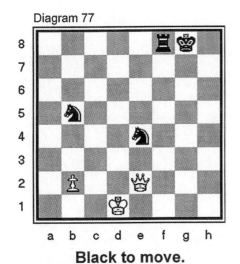

Black to move.

	White	Black
1.	• • •	_____ +
2.	bxc3	_____ +
3.	K moves	_____

To Do Win the White Queen in three moves.

Hint Use a Knight sacrifice check, followed by a Knight Fork check.

Diagram 78

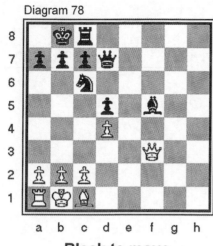

Black to move.

	White	Black
1.	• • •	_____ +
2.	_____	_____ +
3.	K moves	_____

To Do Win the White Queen and two pawns for a Bishop in three moves.

Hint Use a Bishop sacrifice check, followed by a Knight Fork.

Diagram 79

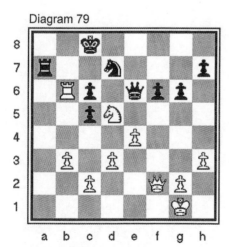

White to move.

	White	Black
1.	_____ +	Q x c6
2.	_____ +	K moves
3.	_____	

To Do Win the Black Queen and a pawn for a Rook and a Knight in three moves.

Hint Use a Rook sacrifice check, followed by a Knight Fork.

3 Knight Forks

Diagram 80

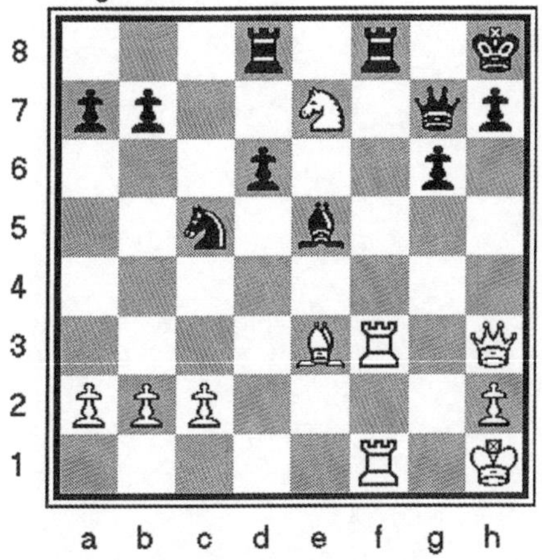

White to move.

	White		Black
1.	_____	+	_____
2.	_____	+	Qxf8
3.	_____	+	K moves
4.	_____		

To Do Win the Black Queen for a Knight in four moves.

Hint Trade Rooks, followed by a Knight Fork check. The Knight Fork is possible because the Black h7 pawn is pinned.

Diagram 81

White to move.

	White		Black
1.	_____	+	Bxd6?
2.	_____	+	K moves
3.	_____		Rhe8
4.	_____		

To Do Win a pawn and the exchange (a Rook for a Knight) in four moves.

Hint Use two Knight checks on d6. Follow those with a Knight move to f7, forking the Black Rooks.

3 Knight Forks

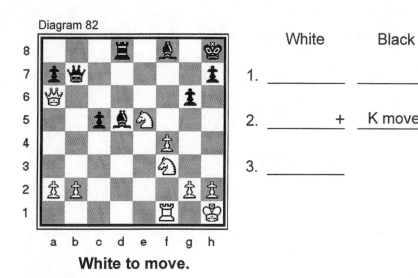

Diagram 82

White to move.

	White	Black
1.	_____	_____
2.	_____ +	K moves
3.	_____	

To Do Win a Rook in three moves.

Hint Trade Queens, and then use a Knight Fork check.

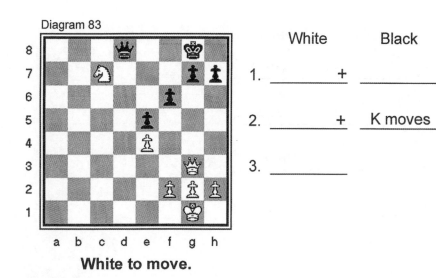

Diagram 83

White to move.

	White	Black
1.	_____ +	_____
2.	_____ +	K moves
3.	_____	

To Do Win a pawn in three moves.

Hint Use a Queen sacrifice check, followed by a Knight Fork.

3 Knight Forks

Diagram 84

White to move.

	White	Black
1.	_____	Qxd5
2.	_____ +	K moves
3.	_____	

To Do Win the Black Bishop in three moves.

Hint Use a Queen sacrifice. Follow that with a Knight Fork, winning back the Queen.

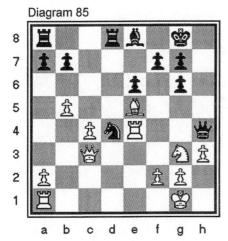

Diagram 85

Black to move.

	White	Black
1.	• • •	_____
2.	Nxe4	_____ +
3.	K moves	_____

To Do Win the White Rook on e4 for a Knight in three moves.

Hint Use a Queen sacrifice, followed by a Knight Fork.

3 Knight Forks

Diagram 86

White to move.

	White	Black
1.	_____	Qxc6?
2.	_____ +	_____
3.	_____	

To Do Win the Black Knight and Bishop in three moves.

Hint Use a Queen sacrifice, followed by a Knight Fork check.

Diagram 87

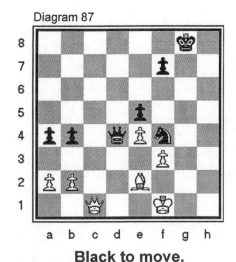

Black to move.

	White	Black
1.	• • •	_____ +
2.	_____	_____ +
3.	K moves	_____

To Do Win the White Bishop in three moves.

Hint Use a Queen sacrifice check, followed by a Knight Fork.

46

3 Knight Forks

Diagram 88

White to move.

	White		Black
1.	_____	+	_____
2.	_____	+	K moves
3.	_____		

To Do Win the Black Rook on c8 in three moves.

Hint Use a Queen sacrifice check, followed by a Knight Fork.

Diagram 89

Black to move.

	White		Black
1.	• • •		_____
2.	g x f3		_____ +
3.	K moves		_____

To Do Win the White Bishop in three moves.

Hint Use a Queen sacrifice, followed by a Knight Fork.

3 Knight Forks

Diagram 90

White to move.

	White	Black
1.	_____	_____
2.	_____ +	K moves
3.	_____	

To Do Win the Black Bishop on c8 in three moves.

Hint Use a Queen sacrifice, followed by a Knight Fork.

Diagram 91

Black to move.

	White	Black
1.	• • • _____	_____ +
2.	_____	_____ +
3.	K moves	_____

To Do Win the White Knight in three moves.

Hint Use a Queen sacrifice check, followed by a Knight Fork, winning back the Queen. The Knight Fork is possible because the f3 pawn is pinned.

48

3 Knight Forks

Diagram 92

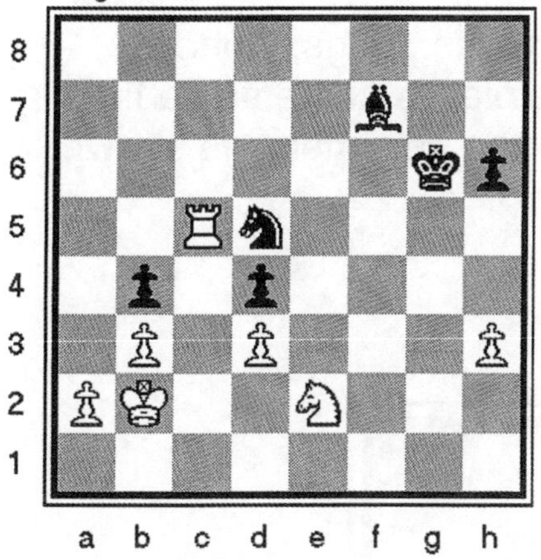

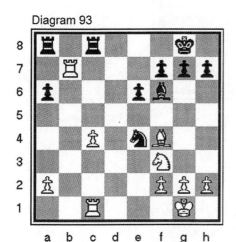

White to move.

	White	Black
1.	_____	_____
2.	_____ +	K moves
3.	_____	

To Do Win the Black Knight and Bishop for a Rook in three moves.

Hint Use a Rook sacrifice, followed by a Knight Fork.

Diagram 93

Black to move.

	White	Black			White	Black
1.	• • •	_____		1.	• • •	_____
2.	Rbb1	_____		2.	Rbb1	_____
3.	Be3	_____		3.	Rc2	_____

To Do On Black's second move, the Black Knight will fork the White Bishop and Rook on c1, winning the exchange or the Bishop in three moves.

Hint Use a Knight attack against the White Rook on b7, followed by a Knight Fork.

49

4 Other Forks/Double Attacks introduction

Other Forks show that any piece can fork—not only Knights. Kings, Queens, Rooks, Bishops, and Pawns can all attack two or more pieces at the same time. Forks are also known as Double Attacks. Some Forks can be simple, as shown in Diagram 94. Others take two or more moves to set up.

Diagram 94

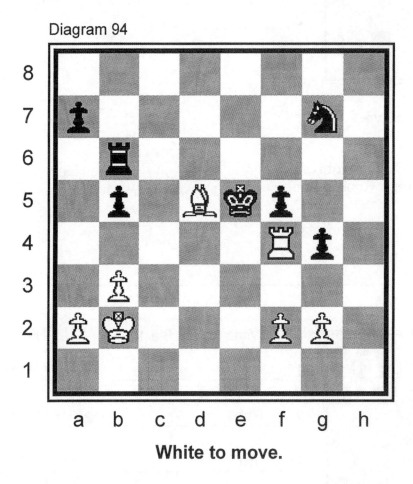

White to move.

Kings can fork! Black just played . . . Ke5, forking the White Rook and Bishop. Whatever White does on the next move, the Black King will capture either the White Rook or Bishop.

Circle the White pieces that are forked by the Black King.

50

4 Other Forks/Double Attacks instruction

Diagram 95

Black to move.

	White	Black		White	Black
1.	• • •	Ke5	1.	• • •	Ke5
2.	B moves	Kxf4	2.	g3	Kxd5

This one is done for you.

 To Do Win the White Bishop or Rook in two moves.

How Black plays . . . Ke5, forking the White Bishop and Rook with the King. Whichever piece White moves, Black can win the other: capturing the Bishop or the Rook.

Diagram 96

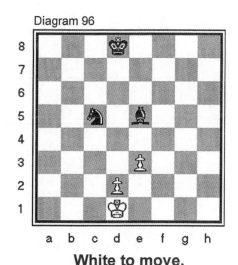

White to move.

	White	Black		White	Black
1.		N moves	1.		Bxd4
2.			2.		

Your turn now!

To Do Win the Black Bishop or Knight in two moves.

How White plays d4, forking the Black Knight and Bishop with the d pawn. Most likely, White will play . . . Bxd4, trading the Bishop for a pawn. This game then ends in a draw.

51

4 Other Forks/Double Attacks instruction

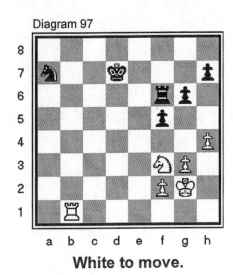

Diagram 97

White to move.

	White	Black
1.	_____ +	K moves
2.	_____	

To Do Win the Black Knight in two moves.

How White plays Rb7+, forking the Black King and Knight with the Rook. Black must move his King. Then, White plays Rxa7, winning the Knight.

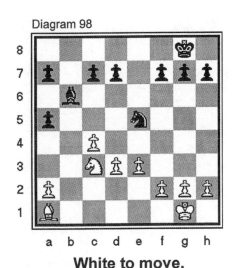

Diagram 98

White to move.

	White	Black		White	Black
1.	_____	Bxc5	1.	_____	Bxc5
2.	_____	Bxd4	2.	_____	N moves
3.	_____		3.	_____	

To Do Win the Black Bishop or Knight for one or two pawns in two moves.

How White plays c5, trapping the Black Bishop. After Black plays . . . Bxc5, White plays d4, forking the Black Bishop and Knight. On the next move White will win the Bishop or the Knight.

52

Diagram 99

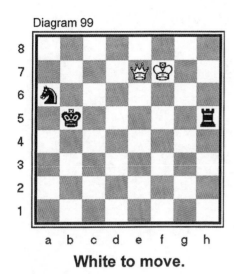

White to move.

White	Black
1. _____ +	K moves
2. _____	

To Do Win the Black Rook in two moves.

Hint Use a Queen Fork.

Diagram 100

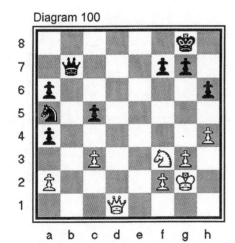

White to move.

White	Black
1. _____ +	_____
2. _____	

To Do Win the Black Knight in two moves.

Hint Use a Queen Fork.

Diagram 101

White to move.

	White		Black
1.		+	K moves
2.			

 To Do Win the Black Rook in two moves.

Hint Use a Queen Fork.

Diagram 102

White to move.

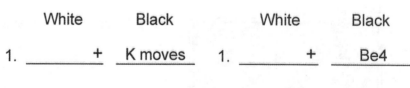

	White		Black		White		Black
1.		+	K moves	1.		+	Be4
2.				2.		+	

 To Do Win the Black Bishop in two moves.

Hint Use a Queen Fork.

4 Other Forks/Double Attacks

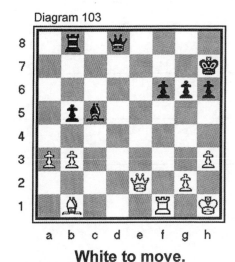

Diagram 103

White to move.

	White	Black
1.	_____ +	Kxg6
2.	_____ +	K moves
3.	_____	

To Do Win the Black pawn on g6.

Hint Use a Bishop sacrifice check, followed by a Queen Fork.

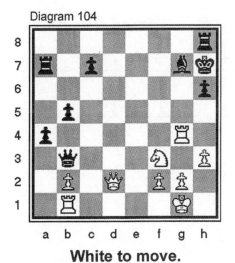

Diagram 104

White to move.

	White	Black
1.	_____ +	Kxg7
2.	_____ +	K moves
3.	_____	

To Do Win the Black Bishop in three moves.

Hint Use a Rook sacrifice check, followed by a Queen Fork.

Diagram 105

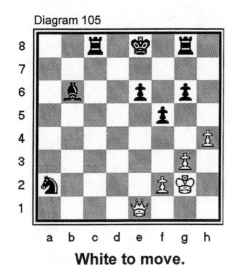

White to move.

White		Black	White		Black
1. _____	+	Kf8	1. _____	+	Kd8
2. _____	+	Kg7	2. _____	+	Kc7
3. _____	+	Kh6	3. _____		
4. _____					

To Do Win a pawn, Rook, and Bishop in four moves (or pawn, Rook, and Knight in three moves!).

Hint Use three Queen Forks!

Diagram 106

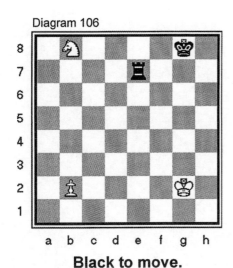

Black to move.

White	Black	White	Black
1. • • • _____	+ _____	1. • • • _____	_____
2. K moves _____		2. N moves _____	

To Do Win the White pawn in two moves.

Hint Use a Rook Fork.

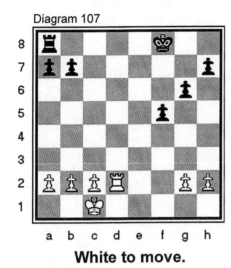

Diagram 107

White to move.

White	Black		White	Black
1. _____	Kg8		1. _____	b6/Rb8
2. _____			2. _____	

To Do Win the b pawn or the h pawn in two moves.

Hint Use a Rook Fork.

Diagram 108

White to move.

White	Black
1. _____ +	K moves
2. _____	

To Do Win the Black g pawn in two moves.

Hint Use a Rook Fork.

Diagram 109

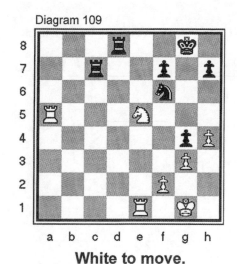

White to move.

	White	Black
1.	_____	Nxg4
2.	_____ +	K moves
3.	_____	

To Do Win the Black g-pawn in three moves.

Hint Use a Knight sacrifice on g4, followed by a Rook Fork.

Diagram 110

White to move.

	White	Black		White	Black
1.	_____	Bxb7	1.	_____	a5?
2.	_____ +	K moves	2.	Nxa5!	Bxa5
3.	_____		3.	Rc5!	Be6
			4.	_____	

To Do Win the Black pawn on b7 in three moves.

Hint Use a Knight sacrifice on b7, followed by a Rook Fork. (If Black plays . . . a5?, White wins two pawns!)

58

4 Other Forks/Double Attacks

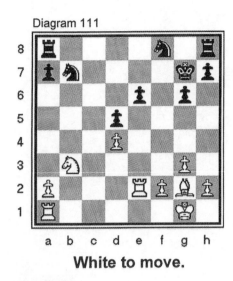

Diagram 111

White to move.

	White	Black
1.	________	exd5
2.	________ +	K moves
3.	________	

To Do Win a pawn in three moves.

Hint Use a Bishop sacrifice (Bxd5), followed by a Rook Fork.

Diagram 112

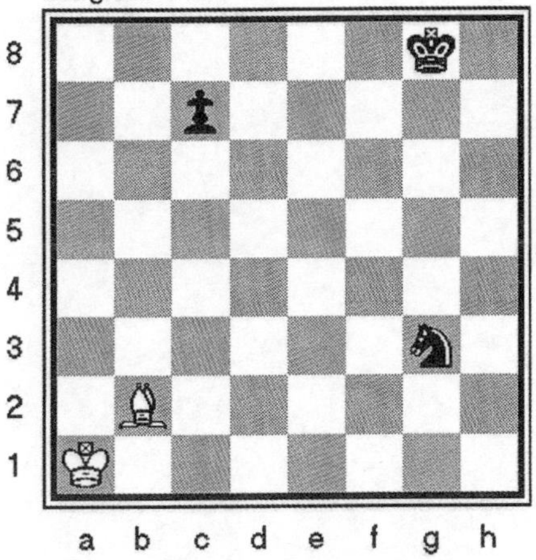

White to move.

	White	Black		White	Black
1.	________	N moves	1.	________	P moves
2.	________		2.	________	

To Do Win the Black pawn or Knight in two moves.

Hint Use a Bishop Fork.

Diagram 113

White to move.

	White	Black
1.	____ +	K moves
2.	____	

To Do Win the Black pawn on c6 and Knight in two moves.

Hint Use a Bishop Fork.

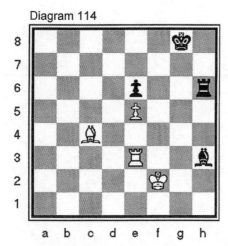

Diagram 114

White to move.

	White	Black
1.	____	Rxh3
2.	____ +	K moves
3.	____	

To Do Win the Black pawn and Bishop in three moves.

Hint Use a Rook sacrifice, followed by a Bishop Fork.

4 Other Forks/Double Attacks

Diagram 115

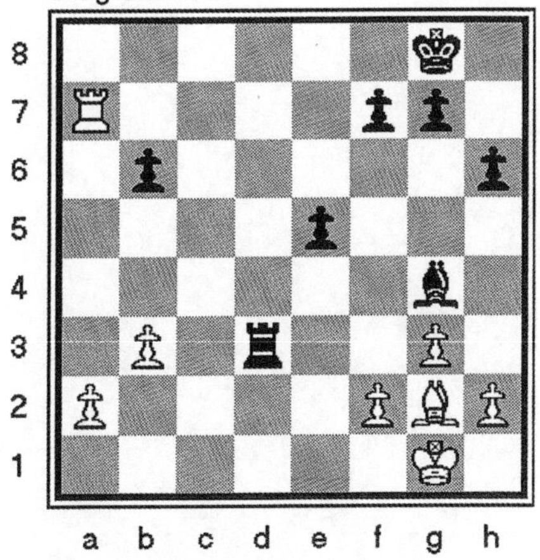

White to move.

	White		Black
1.	_____	+	Kh7 ____
2.	_____	+	f5/g6 ____
3.	_____		

To Do Win the Black Rook in three moves.

Hint Use a Rook check, followed by a Bishop Fork.

Diagram 116

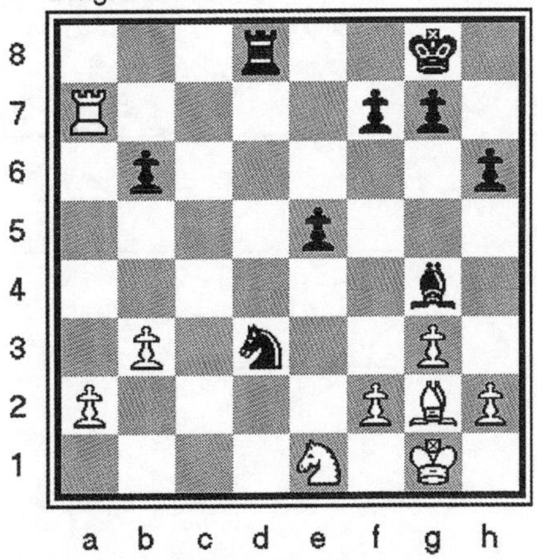

White to move.

	White		Black
1.	_____		Rxd3? ____
2.	_____	+	Kh7 ____
3.	_____	+	f5/g6 ____
4.	_____		

To Do Win the Black Rook in four moves.

Hint Begin by trading Knights. Then, use a Rook check, followed by a Bishop Fork.

61

Diagram 117

Black to move.

	White	Black
1.	• • •	
2.	Rxg3?	+
3.	K moves	

To Do Win the White Bishop in three moves.

Hint Use a Rook sacrifice (. . . Rxg3) followed by a Bishop Fork.

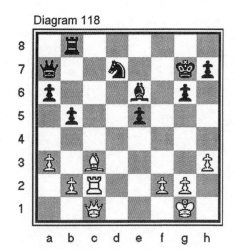

Diagram 118

White to move.

	White	Black		White	Black
1.	+	K moves	1.	+	Nxe5??
2.			2.	+	Qxc7
			3.		

To Do Win the Black e-pawn and Rook for a Bishop in two moves—or win the Black e-pawn and Queen for a Bishop and Rook in three moves.

Hint Use a Bishop fork (check) on e5. Then, if the Black King moves, capture the Rook. If, instead, Black plays . . . Nxe5??, then play Rc7+ and win the Black Queen.

4 Other Forks/Double Attacks

Diagram 119

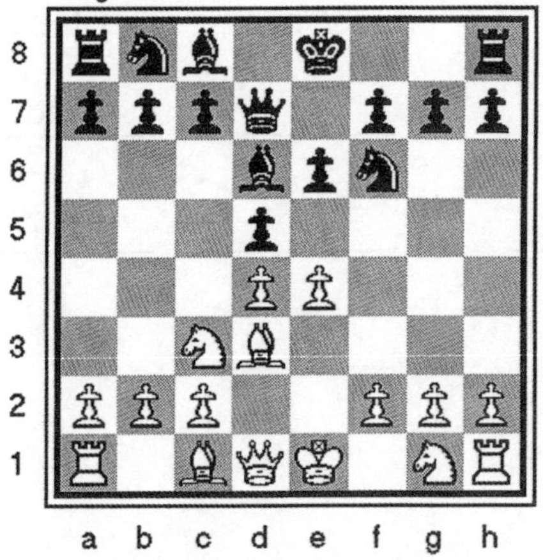

White to move.

White	Black	White	Black
1. _____	Be7	1. _____	Bxe5
2. _____		2. _____	

To Do Win a Black Bishop or Knight in two moves.

Hint Use a Pawn Fork.

Diagram 120

Black to move.

White	Black
1. • • • _____	_____
2. Nf3 _____	_____
3. Q moves _____	_____

To Do Win the Knight on b3 for a pawn in three moves.

Hint Use a pawn push (. . . c5), followed by a Pawn Fork that attacks the White Queen and Knight on b3.

Diagram 121

White to move.

White	Black		White	Black
1. _____	Bd6	1. _____	Bd6
2. _____	N moves	2. _____	Be7
3. _____		3. _____	

To Do Win a Black Bishop or Knight for a pawn in three moves.

Hint Use a Pawn Fork.

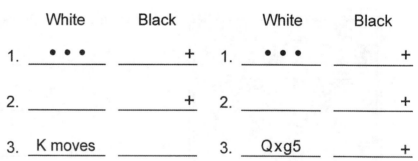

Diagram 122

Black to move.

White	Black		White	Black
1. • • •	_____ +	1. • • •	_____ +
2. _____	_____ +	2. _____	_____ +
3. K moves	_____	3. Qxg5	_____ +

To Do Win the White Queen for a Bishop in three moves.

Hint Use a Bishop sacrifice check, (. . . Bxf4+), followed by a Pawn Fork.

4 Other Forks/Double Attacks

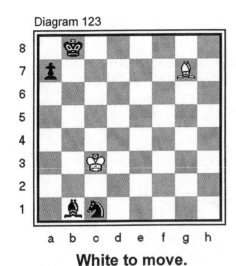

Diagram 123

White to move.

	White	Black	White	Black
1.	_____	N moves	1. _____	B moves
2.	_____		2. _____	

To Do Win a Black Bishop or Knight in two moves.

Hint Use a King Fork.

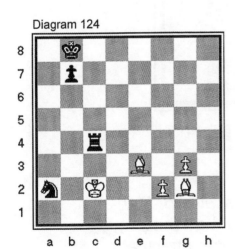

Diagram 124

White to move.

	White	Black	White	Black
1.	_____	Rc3+	1. _____	N moves?
2.	_____		2. _____	

To Do Win the Black Rook or Knight in two moves.

Hint Use a King Fork.

5 Discovered Checks introduction

A **Discovered Check** occurs when a piece moves and uncovers a check on the enemy King. The enemy King *discovers* or finds out it is in check! A Discovered Check may be simple, such as the one shown in Diagram 125. Others take two or more moves to set up.

Diagram 125

White to move.

After White plays Bd3+, Black will *discover* or find out that the Black King is in check by the White Rook, and that the Black Queen is under attack at the same time! When Black moves the King, the White Bishop will capture the Black Queen.

Circle the White piece that will check the Black King.

5 Discovered Checks instruction

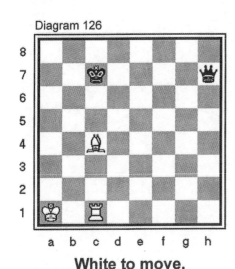

Diagram 126

8 7 6 5 4 3 2 1
a b c d e f g h

White to move.

White	Black	White	Black
1. Bd3 +	K moves	1. Bg8 +	Qc2
2. Bxh7		2. Rxc2 +	

This one is done for you.

 To Do Win the Black Queen in two moves.

How White plays Bd3+ or Bg8+. Black discovers the Black King is in check and that the Black Queen is under attack. On the next move, White wins the Queen.

Diagram 127

8 7 6 5 4 3 2 1
a b c d e f g h

White to move.

White	Black	White	Black
1. _____ +	Kf8	1. _____ +	Be6
2. _____		2. _____ +	

Your turn now!

To Do Win the Black Queen for a Bishop in two moves.

How White plays Bb5+. Black discovers that the Black King is in check by the White Rook on e1. White can play Bxc6 on the next move, winning the Queen for a Bishop.

67

5 Discovered Checks instruction

Diagram 128

White to move.

White		Black
1. _____	+	Kh8 _____
2. _____		

To Do Win a pawn and the Black Knight in two moves.

How White plays Nxe5+, uncovering a check from the White Bishop. After Black plays . . . Kh8, White plays Nxg4, winning a pawn and a Knight!

Diagram 129

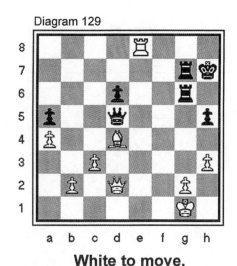

White to move.

White		Black		White		Black
1. _____	+	_____		1. _____	+	_____
2. _____	+	Rxg7		2. _____	+	Kxg7
3. _____				3. _____		

To Do Win the Black Queen for a Bishop in three moves.

How White sacrifices the Rook, playing Rh8+, forcing Black to play . . . Kxh8. White then plays Bxg7+, uncovering an attack on the Black Queen, which White captures on the next move.

5 Discovered Checks

Diagram 130

White to move.

White   Black

1. _____ #

To Do Checkmate in one move.

Hint Use a Bishop move combined with a Discovered Check from the White Rook.

Diagram 131

White to move.

White   Black

1. _____ #

To Do Checkmate in one move.

Hint Use a Bishop move combined with a Discovered Check from the White Queen.

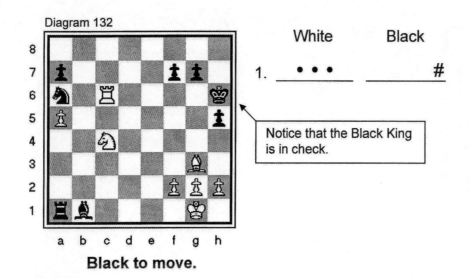

Diagram 132

Black to move.

Notice that the Black King is in check.

	White	Black
1.	• • •	#

To Do Checkmate in one move.

Hint Use a Bishop move combined with a Discovered Check from the Black Rook.

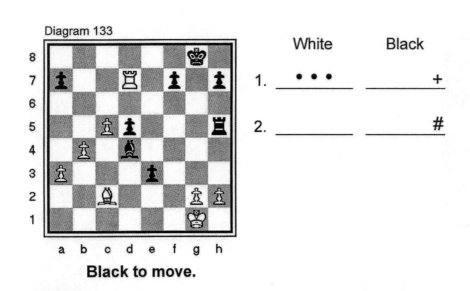

Diagram 133

Black to move.

	White	Black
1.	• • •	+
2.		#

To Do Checkmate in two moves.

Hint Use a pawn push (threatening to promote), combined with a Discovered Check from the Black Bishop.

5 Discovered Checks

Diagram 134

White to move.

	White	Black		White	Black
1.	_____ +	Qf6	1.	_____ +	Kg8??
2.	_____		2.	_____	

To Do Win the Black Queen for a Bishop in two moves.

Hint Use a pawn attack against the Black Queen, combined with a Discovered Check from the White Bishop.

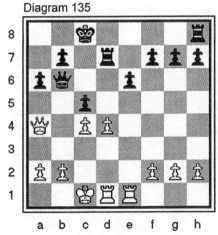

Diagram 135

White to move.

	White	Black		White	Black
1.	_____ +	Kxd7	1.	_____ +	Kxd7
2.	_____ +	Kc6	2.	_____ +	Qd6?
3.	_____		3.	_____	

To Do Win the Black Rook on d7 in three moves.

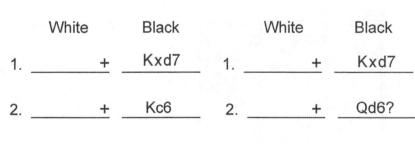

Hint Use a Queen sacrifice check (Qxd7+). Follow that by a pawn attack on the Black Queen, combined with a Discovered Check from the White Rook on d1.

71

5 Discovered Checks

Diagram 136

White to move.

	White	Black		White	Black
1.	_____ +	Ka8	1.	_____ +	Rc7??
2.	_____ +		2.	_____ +	

To Do Win a Black Rook for a pawn in two moves.

Hint Use a pawn push (threatening to Promote or capture the Black Rook), combined with a Discovered Check from the White Queen.

Diagram 137

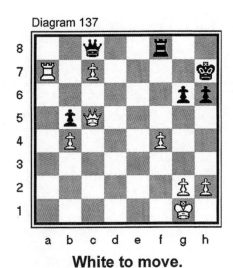

White to move.

	White	Black
1.	_____	Qxf8
2.	_____ +	Kg8
3.	_____ +	

To Do Win the Black Rook for a pawn in three moves.

Hint Use a Queen sacrifice check (Qxf8). Follow that by a pawn push (promoting the pawn), combined with a Discovered Check from the White Rook.

5 Discovered Checks

Diagram 138

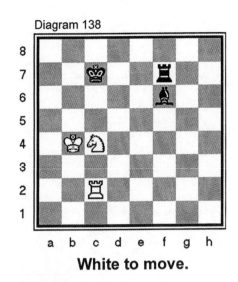

White to move.

	White		Black
1.	_____	+	K moves
2.	_____		

 To Do Win the Black Rook in two moves.

 Hint Use a Knight attack on the Black Rook, combined with a Discovered Check from the White Rook.

Diagram 139

White to move.

	White		Black		White		Black
1.	_____	+	Be7	1.	_____	+	Qe7
2.	_____			2.	_____		

 To Do Win the Black Queen for a Knight in two moves.

Hint Use a Knight attack on the Black Queen, combined with a Discovered Check from the White Queen.

5 Discovered Checks

Diagram 140

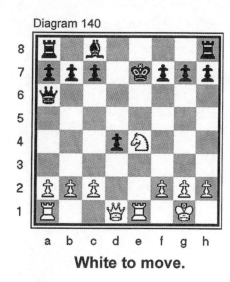

White to move.

White		Black	White		Black
1. _____	+	Qe6	1. _____	+	Be6
2. _____			2. _____		

To Do Win the Black Queen for a Knight in two moves.

Hint Use a Knight attack on the Black Queen, combined with a Discovered Check from the White Rook on e1.

Diagram 141

White to move.

White		Black	White		Black
1. _____	+	K moves/f6	1. _____	+	Qd4/c3/b2?
2. _____	+		2. _____	+	

To Do Win the Black Queen in two moves.

Hint Use a Knight attack on the Black Queen, combined with a Discovered Check from the White Bishop.

5 Discovered Checks

Diagram 142

White to move.

	White	Black		White	Black
1.	_____ +	Kxb7	1.	_____ +	Kxb7
2.	_____ +	K moves	2.	_____ +	Qb3/b4
3.	_____		3.	_____ +	

To Do Win the Black Rook in three moves.

Hint Use a Queen sacrifice check (Qxb7+). Follow this by a Knight attack on the Black Queen, combined with a Discovered Check from the White Rook.

Diagram 143

White to move.

	White	Black
1.	_____ +	Kxh6
2.	_____ +	Any move
3.	_____	

To Do Win a pawn and the Black Queen for a Rook in three moves.

Hint Use a Rook sacrifice check (Rxh6+). Follow this by a Knight attack on the Black Queen, combined with a Discovered Check from the White Queen.

Diagram 144

White to move.

	White	Black		White	Black
1.	_____ +	Kb8	1.	_____ +	Kd8
2.	_____ #		2.	_____ #	

To Do Checkmate in two moves.

Hint Use a Knight move combined with a Discovered Check from the White Bishop on a6. Follow that by a Queen or Knight checkmate.

Diagram 145

White to move.

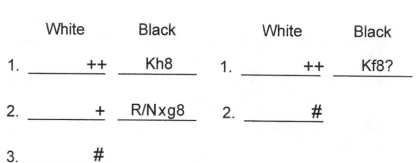

	White	Black		White	Black
1.	_____ ++	Kh8	1.	_____ ++	Kf8?
2.	_____ +	R/Nxg8	2.	_____ #	
3.	_____ #				

To Do Deliver a *smothered checkmate* in three moves.

Hint Use a Knight move combined with a Discovered Check from the White Queen (a double check). Then, use a Queen sacrifice check (Qg8+), followed by a Knight mate.

5 Discovered Checks

Diagram 146

White to move.

	White	Black		White	Black
1.	_____ +	K moves	1.	_____ +	Ne7??
2.	_____		2.	_____ #	

To Do Win the Black Queen or checkmate in two moves.

Hint Use a Bishop attack on the Black Queen, combined with a Discovered Check from the White Queen.

Diagram 147

Black to move.

	White	Black		White	Black
1.	• • • _____	_____ +	1.	• • • _____	_____ +
2.	Qf3 _____	_____ +	2.	K moves? _____	_____

To Do Win the White Queen and a pawn for a Rook in two moves.

Hint Use a Bishop attack on the White Queen, combined with a Discovered Check from the Black Rook on f8.

77

5 Discovered Checks

Diagram 148

White to move.

White		Black		White		Black
1. _____	+	K moves		1. _____	+	Ne7
2. _____				2. _____	+	

To Do Win the Black Knight in two moves.

Hint Use a Bishop attack on the Knight, combined with a Discovered Check from the White Rook.

Diagram 149

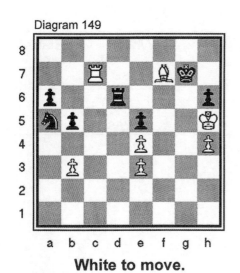

White to move.

White		Black		White		Black
1. _____		Nc6		1. _____		Nb3/c4
2. _____	+	K moves		2. _____	+	
3. _____						

To Do Win the Black Knight in three moves.

Hint Use a pawn attack to force the Knight to move. Then, use a Bishop attack on the Knight, combined with a Discovered Check from the White Rook.

5 Discovered Checks

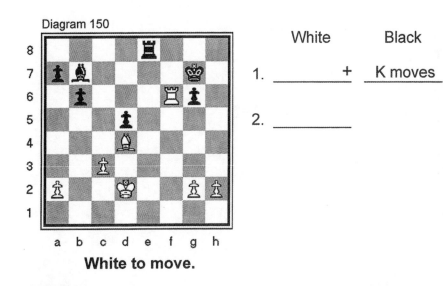

Diagram 150

8 7 6 5 4 3 2 1
a b c d e f g h

White to move.

White	Black
1. _____ +	K moves
2. _____	

To Do Win the Black pawn on b6 and the Bishop in two moves.

Hint Use a Rook attack on the Black Bishop, combined with a Discovered Check from the White Bishop.

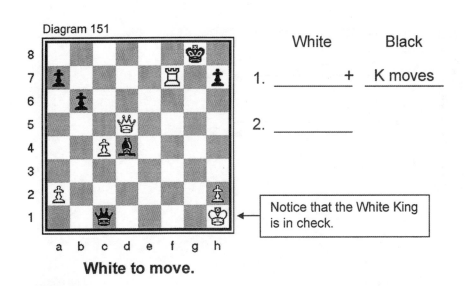

Diagram 151

8 7 6 5 4 3 2 1
a b c d e f g h

White to move.

White	Black
1. _____ +	K moves
2. _____	

Notice that the White King is in check.

To Do Win the Black Queen in two moves.

Hint Use a Rook attack on the Black Queen, combined with a Discovered Check from the White Queen.

79

5 Discovered Checks

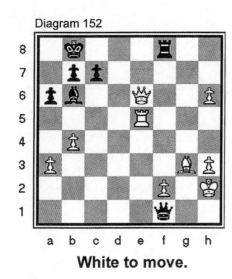

Diagram 152

White to move.

	White	Black
1.	_____	cxb6
2.	_____ +	K moves
3.	_____	

To Do Win the Black Bishop in three moves.

Hint Use a Queen sacrifice (Qxb6!). Follow this by a Rook attack on the Black Queen, combined with a Discovered Check from the White Bishop.

Diagram 153

White to move.

	White	Black
1.	_____ +	_____
2.	Rg8++	_____
3.	_____ #	

To Do Checkmate in three moves.

Hint Use a Rook check (Rxg7+). Then, use a Rook sacrifice double check (Rg8++). Follow this with a mate from the remaining White Rook.

5 Discovered Checks

Diagram 154

White to move.

	White		Black
1.	_____	+	_____
2.	Rg7+		_____
3.	_____	+	_____
4.	_____	+	

Winning pieces by alternately using a Discovered Check and a regular check is known as the "windmill."

 To Do Win both Black Bishops and the Rook in four moves.

Hint Play Rxb7, combined with a Discovered Check from the White Bishop. Follow this by a series of Rook checks, combined with Discovered Checks from the White Bishop.

Diagram 155

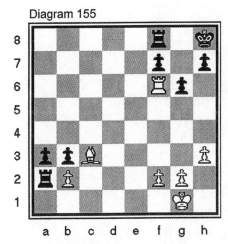

White to move.

	White		Black
1.	_____	+	_____
2.	Rg7+		_____
3.	Rxg6+		_____
4.		#	

To Do Checkmate in four moves.

Hint Play Rxf7, combined with a Discovered Check from the White Bishop. Then, use a Rook check, followed by a Rook capture and Discovered Check. Mate with the White Bishop.

6 Double Checks introduction

A **Double Check** occurs when two pieces attack the King at the same time. The enemy King *discovers* or finds out that it is in check by two pieces at once! Some double checks are simple, as shown in Diagram 156. Others take two or more moves to set up.

Diagram 156

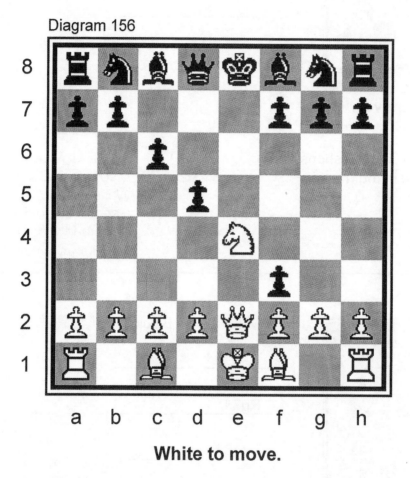

White to move.

White checkmates in one move! White plays the Knight to f6 (Nf6++) and says, "Checkmate." Black then discovers that the Black King is in check by both the White Queen and the White Knight! The Black King is checkmated.

Circle the White pieces that will check the Black King.

6 Double Checks instruction

Diagram 157

White to move.

White	Black
1. **Nf6** #	

This one is done for you.

To Do Checkmate in one move.

How White plays Nf6++ and says "Checkmate." Black *discovers* the Black King is in check by both the White Queen and White Knight. The Black King is checkmated.

Diagram 158

White to move.

White	Black
1. _____ #	

Your turn now!

To Do Checkmate in one move.

How White plays Bb5++ and says "Checkmate." Black *discovers* that the Black King is in check by both the White Rook on e1 and the White Bishop on b5. The Black King is checkmated.

6 Double Checks instruction

Diagram 159

White to move.

	White	Black		White	Black
1.	++	Ke8	1.	++	Kc7
2.	#		2.	#	

To Do Checkmate in two moves.

How White plays Bg5++. The White Bishop on g5 and the White Rook on d1 check the Black King. If Black plays . . . Ke8, White plays Rd8#. If Black plays . . . Kc7, White plays Bd8#.

Diagram 160

White to move.

	White	Black		White	Black
1.	+		1.	+	
2.	++	Ke8	2.	++	Kc7
3.	#		3.	#	

To Do Checkmate in three moves.

How White plays Qd8+! Black must play . . . Kxd8. White plays Bg5 and checks Black's King with the Rook on d1 and the Bishop on g5. White checkmates after Black plays . . . Ke8 or . . . Kc7.

6 Double Checks

Diagram 161

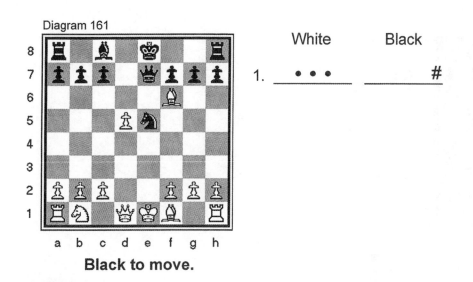

Black to move.

White	Black
1. • • •	____ #

To Do Checkmate in one move.

Hint Use a Double Check from the Black Knight and Black Queen.

Diagram 162

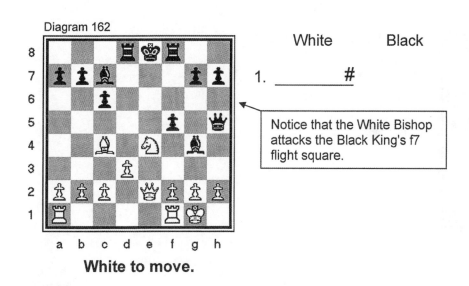

White to move.

White	Black
1. ____ #	

Notice that the White Bishop attacks the Black King's f7 flight square.

To Do Checkmate in one move.

Hint Use a Double Check from the White Knight and White Queen.

6 Double Checks

Diagram 163

White to move.

White	Black
1. _____ #	

To Do Checkmate in one move.

Hint Use a Double Check from the White Knight and White Rook.

Diagram 164

Black to move.

White	Black
1. • • • _____	_____ #

To Do Checkmate in one move.

Hint Use a Double Check from the Black Rook and Black Bishop.

86

6 Double Checks

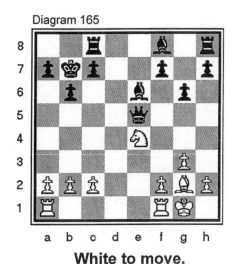

Diagram 165

White to move.

	White	Black
1.	_____ ++	Kb8
2.	_____ #	

To Do Checkmate in two moves.

Hint Use a Double Check from the White Knight and White Bishop. Follow this by a Knight mate.

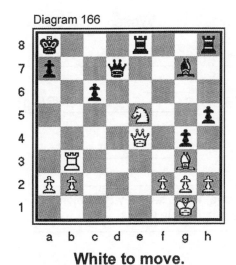

Diagram 166

White to move.

	White	Black		White	Black
1.	_____ +	Kxb8	1.	_____ +	Rxb8
2.	_____ ++		2.	_____	

To Do Win the Black Queen for a Rook in two moves.

Hint Use a Rook sacrifice check (Rb8+). Follow this by a Double Check from the White Knight and White Bishop.

6 Double Checks

Diagram 167

White to move.

	White		Black
1.		+	Kxg7
2.		++	Kg8
3.		#	

To Do Checkmate in three moves.

Hint Use a Queen sacrifice check (Qg7+). Then, use a Double Check from the White Knight and White Bishop, followed by a Knight mate.

Diagram 168

White to move.

	White		Black		White		Black
1.		+		1.		+	
2.		++	Ke8/Kf6	2.		++	Kf6/Kg6
3.		#		3.		#	

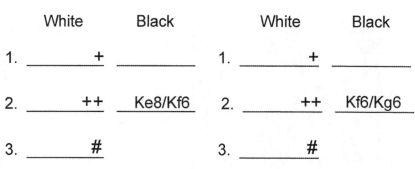

Notice that on the 2nd move, White can play the Knight to either of two squares with Double Check!

To Do Checkmate in three moves.

Hint Use a Bishop sacrifice check (Bxf7+). Then, use a Double Check from the White Knight and White Queen, followed by a Queen checkmate.

6 Double Checks

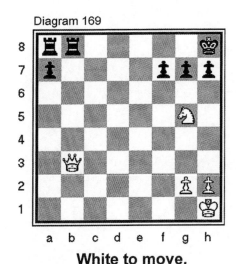

Diagram 169

White to move.

	White	Black		White	Black
1.	_____ +	Kg8	1.	_____ +	Kg8
2.	_____ ++	Kh8	2.	_____ ++	Kf8?
3.	Qg8+! _____		3.	_____ #	
4.	_____ #				

To Do Checkmate in four moves— or three moves if Black plays . . . Kf8?

Hint Use a Knight check (Nxf7+). Next, use a Double Check from the White Knight and White Queen. Now, play Qg8+!, sacrificing the Queen, followed by a smothered mate from the Knight.

Diagram 170

White to move.

	White	Black
1.	_____ +	_____
2.	_____ ++	Kh8
3.	_____ #	

To Do Checkmate in three moves.

Hint Use a Queen sacrifice check (Qxh7+). Then, use a Double Check from the White Knight and White Bishop, followed by a Knight checkmate.

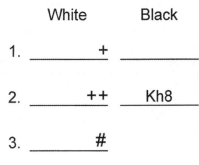

6 Double Checks

Diagram 171

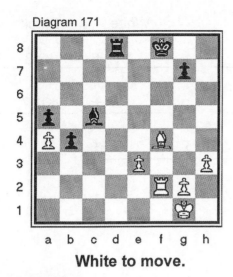

White to move.

	White	Black
1.	_____ ++	K moves
2.	_____	

To Do Win the Black Bishop in two moves.

Hint Use a Double Check from the White Bishop and White Rook.

Diagram 172

Black to move.

	White	Black
1.	• • •	_____ ++
2.	Ke1	_____ #

To Do Checkmate in two moves.

Hint Use a Double Check from the Black Bishop and Black Rook, followed by a Rook mate.

6 Double Checks

Diagram 173

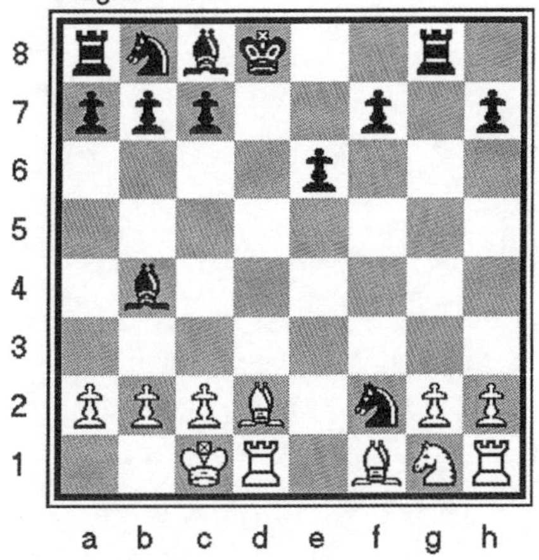

White to move.

	White	Black
1.	++	
2.	#	

To Do Checkmate in two moves.

Hint Use a Double Check from the White Bishop and White Rook, followed by a Rook mate!

Diagram 174

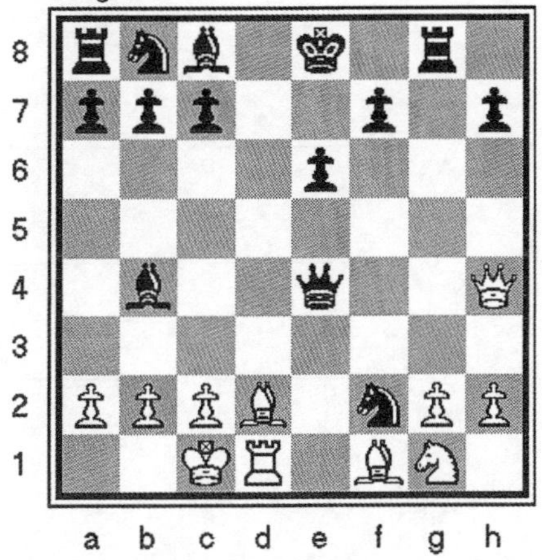

White to move.

	White	Black
1.	+	
2.	++	
3.	#	

To Do Checkmate in three moves.

Hint Use a Queen sacrifice check (Qd8+). Then, use a Double Check from the White Bishop and White Rook, followed by a Rook mate!

91

6 Double Checks

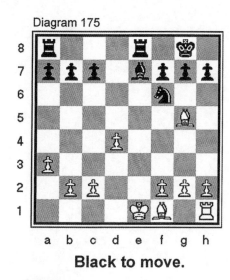

Diagram 175

Black to move.

	White	Black
1.	• • •	++
2.		#

To Do Checkmate in two moves.

Hint Use a Double Check from the Black Bishop and Black Rook, followed by a Rook mate.

Diagram 176

Black to move.

	White	Black		White	Black
1.	• • •		1.	• • •	
2.	Bd3!	(Q move)	2.	exd4??	++
			3.		#

To Do Win a Rook in one move or checkmate in three moves.

Hint Use a Queen sacrifice (Qxd4). Then, if White plays exd4??, use a Double Check from the Black Bishop and Black Rook, followed by a Rook mate!

92

6 Double Checks

Diagram 177

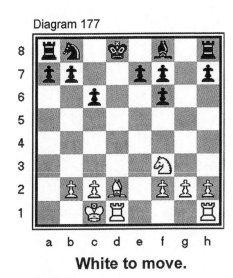

White to move.

	White	Black
1.	_____ ++	Kc8/Ke8
2.	_____ #	

To Do Checkmate in two moves.

Hint Use a Double Check from the White Bishop and White Rook, followed by a Rook mate!

Diagram 178

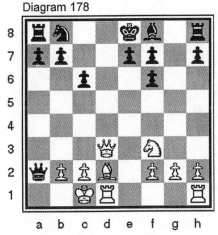

White to move.

	White	Black
1.	_____ +	_____
2.	_____ ++	Kc8/Ke8
3.	_____ #	

To Do Checkmate in three moves.

Hint Use a Queen sacrifice check (Qd8+). Then, use a Double Check from the White Bishop and White Rook, followed by a Rook mate!

6 Double Checks

Diagram 179

White to move.

	White	Black
1.	_____ ++	_____
2.	_____ #	

To Do Checkmate in two moves.

Hint Use a Double Check from the White Bishop and White Rook, followed by a Rook mate.

Diagram 180

	White	Black
1.	_____ +	_____
2.	_____ ++	_____
3.	_____ #	

Black to move.

To Do Checkmate in three moves.

Hint Use a Queen sacrifice check (Qd8+). Then, use a Double Check from the White Bishop and the White Rook, followed by a Rook mate.

94

6 Double Checks

Diagram 181

White to move.

	White		Black
1.	_____	+	_____
2.	_____	#	

To Do Checkmate in two moves.

Hint Use a Knight sacrifice check (Nf5+). Then, use a Double Check and mate from the White Bishop and White Rook.

Diagram 182

White to move.

	White		Black		White		Black
1.	_____	+	Bxf6?	1.	_____	+	Qxf6
2.	_____	#		2.	Qd8+!		_____
				3.	_____	#	

To Do Checkmate in two or three moves.

Hint Use a Knight sacrifice check (Nf6+). Then, depending on Black's move, use a Bishop and Rook Double Check and mate *or* use a Queen sacrifice check, followed by a Double Check and mate from the Bishop and Rook.

95

6 Double Checks

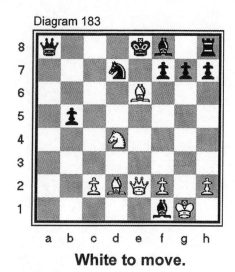

Diagram 183

White to move.

White		Black	White		Black
1. _____	++	Kd8	1. _____	++	Kxf7??
2. _____	+	_____	2. _____	#	
3. _____					

To Do Win the Black Queen in three moves, or checkmate in two moves.

Hint Use a Double Check from the White Bishop and White Queen (Bxf7++!), followed by winning the Black Queen, or delivering a Queen checkmate.

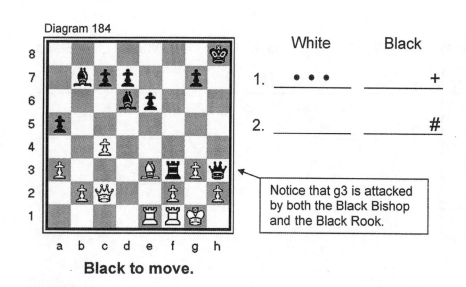

Diagram 184

Notice that g3 is attacked by both the Black Bishop and the Black Rook.

Black to move.

White		Black
1. • • •		_____ +
2. _____		_____ #

To Do Checkmate in two moves.

Hint Use a Queen sacrifice check (. . .Qg2+). Then, use a Double Check and mate from the Black Rook and Black Bishop.

6 Double Checks

Diagram 185

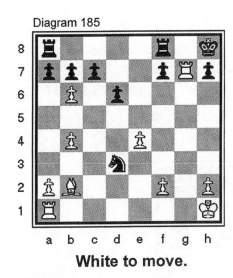

White to move.

	White	Black
1.	++	Kxg8
2.	#	

To Do Checkmate in two moves.

Hint Use a Double Check from the White Rook and White Bishop (a Rook sacrifice!). Next, deliver checkmate with the remaining Rook.

Diagram 186

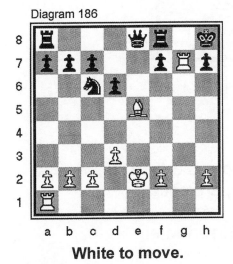

White to move.

	White	Black
1.	++	Kxg8
2.	#	

To Do Checkmate in two moves.

Hint Use a Double Check from the White Rook and White Bishop (a Rook sacrifice!). Next, deliver checkmate with the remaining Rook.

7 Discovered Attacks introduction

A **Discovered Attack** occurs when a piece moves and uncovers an attack by a piece behind it. Both pieces attack different enemy pieces at the same time. Some Discovered Attacks are simple, as shown in Diagram 187. Others take two or more moves to set up.

Diagram 187

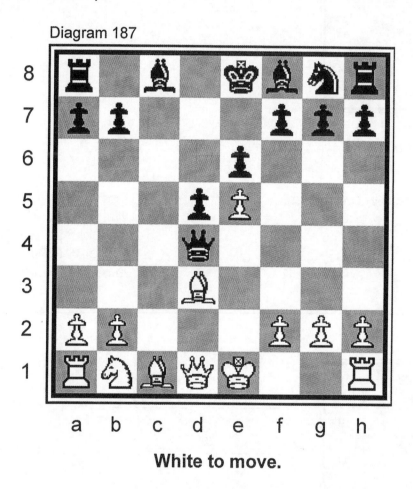

White to move.

When White plays Bb5+, Black *discovers* or find out that that the Queen and the King are both under attack at the same time. After dealing with the Bishop check, Black loses the Queen when White plays Qxd4!

Circle the White pieces that will win Black's Queen.

7 Discovered Attacks instruction

Diagram 188

White to move.

	White	Black		White	Black
1.	Bb5 +	Ke7	1.	Bb5 +	Bd7
2.	Qxd4		2.	Bxd7 +	Kxd7
			3.	Qxd4	

This one is done for you.

 To Do Win the Black Queen in two or three moves.

 How White plays Bb5+, attacking both Black's King and Queen. If Black moves the King, White plays Qxd4, winning the Black Queen. If Black plays . . . Be7, White plays Bxd7+ and then Qxd4.

Diagram 189

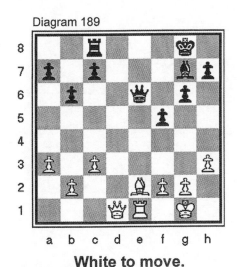

White to move.

	White	Black
1.	_____	Q moves
2.	_____	

Your turn now!

 To Do Win the Black Rook in two moves.

 How White plays Ba6, attacking the Black Rook, and uncovering an attack on the Black Queen from the White Rook. After Black moves the Queen, White plays Bxc8, winning the Rook.

7 Discovered Attacks instruction

Diagram 190

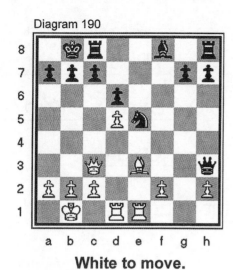

White to move.

	White		Black
1.	_____	+	Kxa7/Ka8
2.	_____		

To Do Win the Black Queen and a pawn for a Bishop in two moves.

How White plays Bxa7+, attacking both Black's King and Queen. After Black plays . . . Kxa7 or . . . Ka8, White plays Qxh3, winning Black's Queen.

Diagram 191

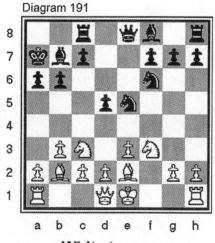

White to move.

	White		Black
1.	_____		Qxe5??
2.	_____	+	axb5
3.	_____		

To Do Win the Black Queen for a Knight in three moves.

How White first trades Knights (Nxe5) and Black plays . . . Qxe5?? Then, White plays Nb5+ and attacks the Black Queen with the Bishop on b2. After Black plays . . . axb5, White plays Bxe5!

7 Discovered Attacks

Diagram 192

White to move.

	White	Black
1.	_____	Q moves
2.	_____	

To Do Win the Black Bishop for a pawn in two moves.

Hint Use a pawn attack on the Black Bishop, combined with a Discovered Attack against the Black Queen from the White Bishop.

Diagram 193

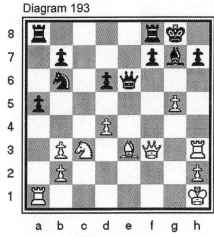

White to move.

	White	Black		White	Black
1.	_____	Q moves	1.	_____	Nxd5
2.	_____		2.	_____	

To Do Win the Black Knight in two moves.

Hint Use a pawn attack on the Black Queen, combined with a Discovered Attack against the Black Knight from the White Bishop.

7 Discovered Attacks

Diagram 194

Black to move.

	White	Black		White	Black
1.	• • •	_____ +	1.	• • •	_____ +
2.	Bxg4	_____	2.	K moves	_____

To Do   Win the White Queen for a Knight in two moves.

Hint   Use a Knight sacrifice check, combined with a Discovered Attack on the White Queen from the Black Bishop.

Diagram 195

Black to move.

	White	Black
1.	• • •	_____
2.	Qxd4??	_____ +
3.	Bxg4	_____

To Do   Win a White Bishop and Queen for a Rook and Knight in three moves.

Hint   Use a Rook sacrifice (. . . Rxd4) —inviting the White Queen to d4. Follow this with a Knight sacrifice check, combined with a Discovered Attack on the White Queen from the Black Bishop.

7 Discovered Attacks

Diagram 196

White to move.

	White		Black
1.	_____	+	g x h6
2.	_____		

To Do Win the Black Queen for a Knight in two moves.

Hint Use a Knight sacrifice check, combined with a Discovered Attack on the Black Queen from the White Queen.

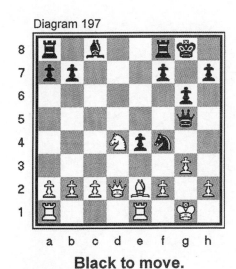

Diagram 197

Black to move.

	White	Black
1.	• • •	_____ +
2.	K moves	_____

To Do Win the White Queen in two moves.

Hint Use a Knight check, combined with a Discovered Attack on the White Queen from the Black Queen.

103

7 Discovered Attacks

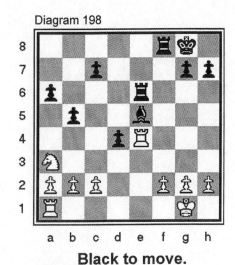

Diagram 198

Black to move.

	White	Black
1.	• • •	+
2.	Kxh2	

To Do Win a White Rook and a pawn for a Bishop in two moves.

Hint Use a Bishop sacrifice check, combined with a Discovered Attack on the White Rook on e4 from the Black Rook on e6.

Diagram 199

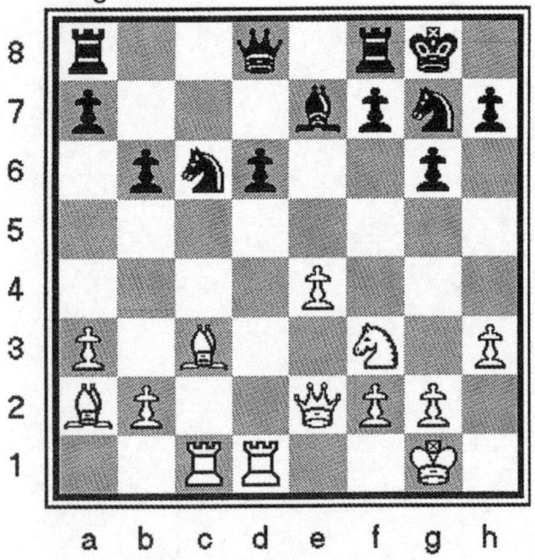

White to move.

	White	Black
1.		Kxg7
2.		

To Do Win the Black Knight on c6 in two moves.

Hint Use a Bishop and Knight trade (Bxg7), combined with a Discovered Attack on the Black Knight on c6 from the White Rook on c1.

7 Discovered Attacks

Diagram 200

White to move.

White	Black
1. _____	R moves
2. _____	

To Do Win the Black Bishop in two moves.

Hint Use a Bishop attack on the Black Rook, combined with a Discovered Attack on the Black Bishop from the White Rook.

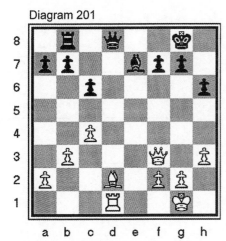

Diagram 201

White to move.

White	Black	White	Black
1. _____	Q moves	1. _____	Bd6?
2. _____		2. _____	

To Do Win the Black Rook for a Bishop in two moves.

Hint Use a Bishop attack on the Black Rook, combined with a Discovered Attack on the Black Queen from the White Rook.

Diagram 202

White to move.

	White		Black
1.	_____	+	Kxh7
2.	_____		

To Do Win the Black Queen and a pawn for a Bishop and a Rook in two moves.

Hint Use a Bishop sacrifice check, combined with a Discovered Attack on the Black Queen from the White Rook on d1.

Diagram 203

White to move.

	White		Black		White		Black
1.	_____	+	K moves	1.	_____	+	Be6?
2.	_____			2.	_____	+	Qxe6
				3.	_____		

To Do Win a Black Rook in two moves.

Hint Use a Bishop check, combined with a Discovered Attack on the Black Rook on a7 from the White Rook on a5.

7 Discovered Attacks

Diagram 204

8 ... White to move.

	White	Black
1.	_____	R x e4
2.	_____	

White to move.

To Do Win the Black Queen for a Rook in two moves.

Hint Use a Bishop attack on the Black Queen, combined with a Discovered Attack (threatening mate!) on the Black Rook.

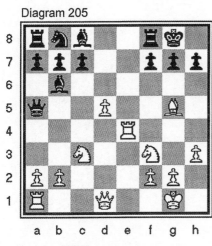

Diagram 205

White to move.

	White	Black
1.	_____	Re8?
2.	_____	Rxe4
3.	_____	

To Do Win the Black Queen for a Rook in three moves.

Hint Use a Bishop attack on the Black Rook on f8. Follow this with a Bishop attack on the Black Queen, combined with a Discovered Attack (threatening mate!) on the Black Rook.

107

7 Discovered Attacks

Diagram 206

White to move.

White		Black
1. _____	+	K/N x h7
2. _____		

To Do Win the Black Queen for a Bishop in two moves.

Hint Use a Bishop sacrifice check, combined with a Discovered Attack on the Black Queen from the White Queen.

Diagram 207

White to move.

White		Black
1. _____	+	Kxf7
2. _____		

To Do Win the Black Queen and a pawn for a Bishop in two moves.

Hint Use a Bishop sacrifice check, combined with a Discovered Attack on the Black Queen from the White Queen.

7 Discovered Attacks

Diagram 208

White to move.

	White		Black
1.	_____	+	B x e6
2.	_____		

To Do Win the Black Queen and a pawn for a Bishop in two moves.

Hint Use a Bishop sacrifice check, combined with a Discovered Attack on the Black Queen from the White Queen.

Diagram 209

White to move.

	White		Black
1.	_____		Q x c7 ??
2.	_____	+	B x e6
3.	_____		

To Do Win the Black Queen and two pawns for a Knight and Bishop in three moves.

Hint Use a Knight sacrifice (N x c7). Follow this with a Bishop sacrifice check, combined with a Discovered Attack on the Black Queen from the White Queen.

Diagram 210

White to move.

	White	Black
1.	_____ +	K moves
2.	_____	

To Do Win the Black Queen in two moves.

Hint Use a Bishop check, combined with a Discovered Attack on the Black Queen from the White Queen.

Diagram 211

White to move.

	White	Black
1.	_____ +	Kxc8
2.	_____ +	K moves
3.	_____	

To Do Win the Black Queen and a Bishop for a Rook in three moves.

Hint Use a Rook sacrifice check. Follow this with a Bishop check, combined with a Discovered Attack on the Black Queen from the White Queen.

110

7 Discovered Attacks

Diagram 212

Black to move.

	White	Black
1.	• • •	_____ +
2.	Kxh2	_____

To Do Win the White Queen and a pawn for a Bishop in two moves.

Hint Use a Bishop sacrifice check, combined with a Discovered Attack on the White Queen from the Black Queen.

Diagram 213

Black to move.

	White	Black		White	Black
1.	• • •	_____	1.	• • •	_____
2.	Qxa6?	_____ +	2.	Qc2	_____
3.	Kxh2	_____			

To Do Win the White Queen and a pawn for two Bishops in three moves—or win a Rook for a Bishop in two moves.

Hint Use a Bishop sacrifice (. . . Ba6!). Follow this with a Bishop sacrifice check, combined with a Discovered Attack on the White Queen from the Black Queen.

7 Discovered Attacks

Diagram 214

White to move.

	White	Black
1.	_____	Kxf7
2.	_____	

 To Do Win the Black Queen and a pawn for a Bishop in two moves.

Hint Use a Bishop sacrifice check, combined with a Discovered Attack on the Black Queen from the White Queen.

Diagram 215

Black to move.

	White	Black
1.	• • •	_____
2.	Q moves	_____

 To Do Win the White Bishop on a3 in two moves.

Hint Use a pawn attack on the White Queen, combined with a Discovered Attack on the White Bishop from the Black Bishop on e7.

112

7 Discovered Attacks

Diagram 216

White to move.

	White	Black
1.	_____ +	Rxe8
2.	_____	

To Do Win the Black Queen for a Rook in two moves.

Hint Use a Rook sacrifice check, combined with a Discovered Attack on the Black Queen from the White Queen.

Diagram 217

White to move.

	White	Black		White	Black
1.	_____	Nf moves	1.	_____	Nd moves
2.	_____		2.	_____	

To Do Win a Black Knight in two moves.

Hint Use a King attack on the Knight on f3 (Ke3), combined with a Discovered Attack on the other Black Knight from the White Rook.

113

8 Skewers introduction

A **Skewer** is an attack on two pieces lined up on the same file, rank, or diagonal. When the first piece moves, a less valuable piece behind it is captured. Some skewers are simple, as shown in Diagram 218. Others take two or more moves to set up.

Diagram 218

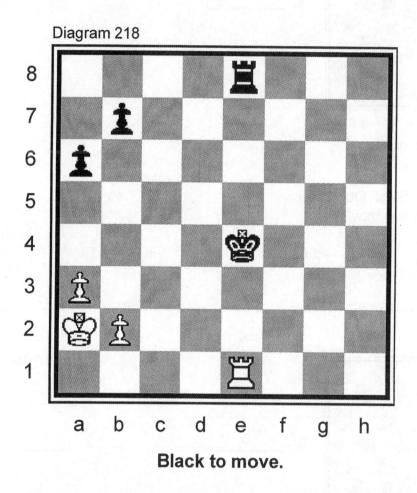

Black to move.

White just played Re1+. Black is in check by the White Rook and must move the King. The Black Rook behind the King is *skewered* and will be captured.

Circle the White piece that will win Black's Rook.

8 Skewers instruction

Diagram 219

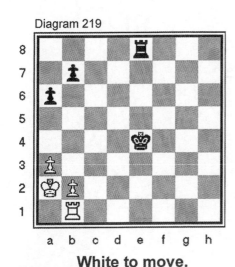

White to move.

	White	Black
1.	Re1 +	K moves
2.	Rxe8	

This one is done for you.

To Do Win the Black Rook in two moves.

How White plays Re1+, skewering the Black Rook. After Black moves the King (. . . K moves), White plays Rxe8, winning the Rook!

Diagram 220

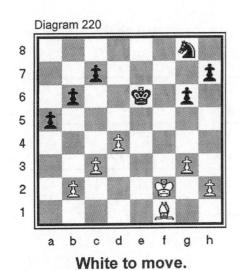

White to move.

	White	Black
1.	_____ +	K moves
2.	_____	

Your turn now!

To Do Win the Black Knight in two moves.

How White plays Bc4+, skewering the Black Knight. Black moves the King (. . . K moves), and White plays Bxg8, winning the Knight!

8 Skewers instruction

Diagram 221

White to move.

	White	Black
1.	_____	R moves
2.	_____	

To Do Win the Black Knight in two moves.

How White plays Qe4, attacking the Black Rook and skewering the Black Knight on b7! When Black moves the Rook, White plays Qxb7, winning the Knight.

Diagram 222

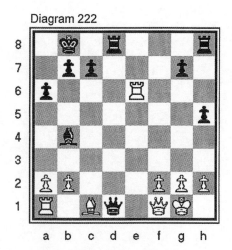

Black to move.

	White	Black		White	Black
1.	• • •	_____ +	1.	• • •	_____ +
2.	Kxf1	_____ +	2.	Kxf1	_____ +
3.	Ke2	_____ +	3.	Re1??	_____ #
4.	K moves	_____			

To Do Win the White Rook on e6 in four moves.

How Black plays . . . Qxf1+, forcing White to play Kxf1. Next, Black plays . . . Rd1+, forcing Ke2. Then, Black plays Re1+, skewering the White Rook on e6, and winning it on the next move (. . . Rxe6).

116

8 Skewers

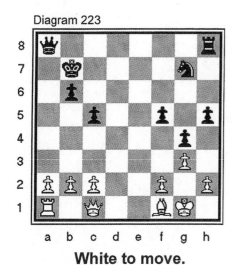

Diagram 223

White to move.

	White	Black
1.	_____ +	K moves
2.	_____	

To Do Win the Black Queen for a Bishop in two moves.

Hint Use a Bishop Skewer, attacking the Black King and the Queen behind it.

Diagram 224

White to move.

	White	Black
1.	_____ +	K moves
2.	_____	

To Do Win a Black Bishop in two moves.

Hint Use a Bishop Skewer, attacking the Black King and the Bishop behind it.

117

Diagram 225

Black to move.

	White	Black
1.	• • •	+
2.	K moves	

To Do Win a Rook in two moves.

Hint Use a Bishop Skewer, attacking the White King and the Rook behind it.

Diagram 226

Black to move.

	White	Black
1.	• • •	
2.	K×d2	+
3.	K moves	

To Do Win a Bishop in three moves.

Hint Begin with a Rook sacrifice (. . . R×d2). Follow this with a Bishop Skewer, attacking the White King and the White Rook behind it.

Diagram 227

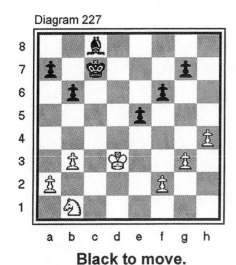

Black to move.

	White	Black
1.	• • •	_____ +
2.	K moves	_____

To Do Win the White Knight in two moves.

Hint Use a Bishop Skewer, attacking the White King and the Knight behind it.

Diagram 228

Black to move.

	White	Black
1.	• • •	_____ +
2.	Kxf3	_____ +
3.	K moves	_____

To Do Win the White Bishop in three moves.

Hint Begin with a Rook sacrifice check. Follow this with a Bishop Skewer, attacking the White King and the Rook behind it.

119

8 Skewers

Diagram 229

White to move.

	White	Black
1.	_____	Q moves
2.	_____	

To Do Win a Black Rook for a Bishop (the exchange) in two moves.

Hint Use a Bishop Skewer, attacking the Black Queen and the Rook behind it.

Diagram 230

White to move.

	White	Black
1.	_____	dxe5
2.	_____	Q moves
3.	_____	

To Do Win a Black Rook for a Bishop (the exchange) in three moves.

Hint Begin with a pawn trade (dxe5). Follow this with a Bishop Skewer, attacking the Black Queen and the Rook behind it.

120

Diagram 231

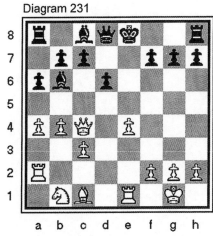

8 | | | | | | | | |
a b c d e f g h

Black to move.

	White	Black
1.	• • •	
2.	Qe2	

To Do Win a White Rook for a Bishop in two moves.

Hint Use a Bishop Skewer, attacking the White Queen and the Rook behind it.

Diagram 232

a b c d e f g h

Black to move.

	White	Black
1.	• • •	
2.	Qxc4	
3.	Qe2	

To Do Win a White Rook for a Bishop in three moves.

Hint Begin with a Knight and Bishop trade (. . . Nxc4). Follow this with a Bishop Skewer, attacking the White Queen and the Rook behind it.

8 Skewers

Diagram 233

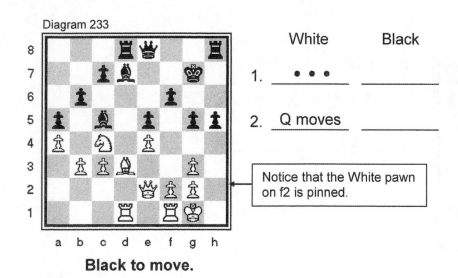

Black to move.

	White	Black
1.	• • •	_____
2.	Q moves	_____

> Notice that the White pawn on f2 is pinned.

To Do Win a White Rook for a Bishop in two moves.

Hint Use a Bishop Skewer, attacking the White Queen and the Rook behind it.

Diagram 234

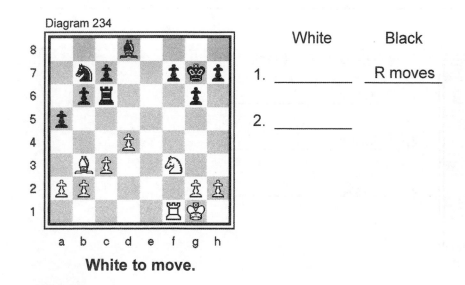

White to move.

	White	Black
1.	_____	R moves
2.	_____	

To Do Win the Black Knight in two moves.

Hint Use a Bishop Skewer, attacking the Black Rook and the Knight behind it.

8 Skewers

Diagram 235

White to move.

	White	Black		White	Black
1.	_____	Rdd8	1.	_____	Rfd8
2.	_____		2.	_____	

To Do Win a Black Rook for a Bishop in two moves.

Hint Use a Bishop Skewer, attacking both Black Rooks.

Diagram 236

White to move.

	White	Black		White	Black
1.	_____	Rgh6	1.	_____	Rhg5
2.	_____		2.	_____	

To Do Win the Black Rook for a Bishop in two moves.

Hint Use a Bishop Skewer, attacking both Black Rooks

123

8 Skewers

Diagram 237

White to move.

	White	Black		White	Black
1.		Rcd7	1.		Rdc8
2.			2.		

 To Do Win a Black Rook for a Bishop in two moves.

 Hint Use a Bishop Skewer, attacking both Black Rooks.

Diagram 238

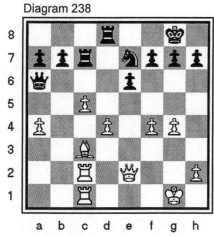

White to move.

	White	Black		White	Black
1.		bxa6	1.		bxa6
2.		Rcd7	2.		Rdc8
3.			3.		

To Do Win a Black Rook for a Bishop in three moves.

 Hint Begin with a Queen trade (Qxa6). Follow this with a Bishop Skewer, attacking both Black Rooks.

Diagram 239

White to move.

White		Black
1. _____	+	K moves
2. _____		

 To Do Win the Black Queen in two moves.

 Hint Use a Rook Skewer, attacking the Black King and the Queen behind it.

Diagram 240

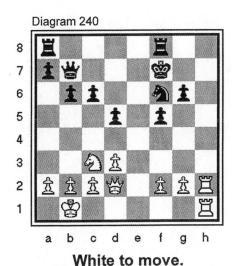

White to move.

White		Black
1. _____	+	N×h7
2. _____	+	K moves
3. _____		

To Do Win the Black Queen and Knight for a Rook in three moves.

 Hint Begin with a Rook sacrifice check. Follow this with a Rook Skewer, attacking the Black King and the Queen behind it.

Diagram 241

White to move.

White	Black
1. _____	Q moves
2. _____	

To Do Win the Black Bishop in two moves.

Hint Use a Rook Skewer, attacking the Black Queen and the Bishop behind it.

Diagram 242

White to move.

White	Black
1. _____	Q moves
2. _____	

To Do Win the Black Knight in two moves.

Hint Use a Rook Skewer, attacking the Black Queen and the Knight behind it.

8 Skewers

Diagram 243

White to move.

	White	Black
1.	_____	dxe5?
2.	_____ +	K moves
3.	_____	

To Do Win the Black Knight and Queen for two Rooks in three moves.

Hint Begin with a Rook sacrifice (Rxe5). Follow this with a Rook Skewer, attacking the Black King and the Queen behind it.

Diagram 244

Black to move.

	White	Black
1.	• • •	_____ +
2.	Bxc6	_____ +
3.	K moves	_____

To Do Win the White Queen for a Knight in three moves.

Hint Begin with a Knight sacrifice check, forking the White King and Queen. Follow this with a Rook Skewer, attacking the White King and the Queen behind it.

8 Skewers

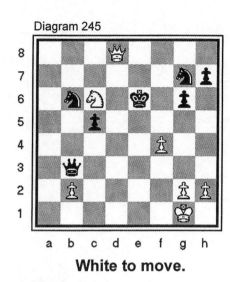

Diagram 245

White to move.

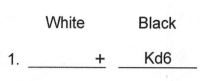

White		Black
1. _____	+	Kd6
2. _____		

To Do Win the Black Queen for a Knight in two moves.

Hint Use a Queen Skewer, attacking the Black King and the Queen behind it.

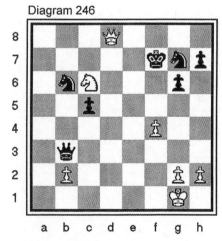

Diagram 246

White to move.

White		Black
1. _____	+	_____
2. _____	+	K moves
3. _____		

To Do Win the Black Queen in three moves.

Hint Begin with a Knight check. Follow this with a Queen Skewer, attacking the Black King and the Queen behind it.

8 Skewers

Diagram 247

	White	Black
1.	_____ +	K moves
2.	_____	

White to move.

To Do Win the Black Queen in two moves.

Hint Use a Queen Skewer, attacking the Black King and the Queen behind it.

Diagram 248

	White	Black
1.	_____ +	K moves
2.	_____	

White to move.

To Do Win the Black Rook in two moves.

Hint Use a Queen Skewer, attacking the Black King and the Rook behind it.

9 Double Threats introduction

A **Double Threat**, as used in this chapter, is a move that threatens to checkmate *or* to win a piece. To avoid checkmate, the opponent must give up the threatened piece. Some Double Threats are simple, as shown in Diagram 249. Others take two or more moves to set up.

Diagram 249

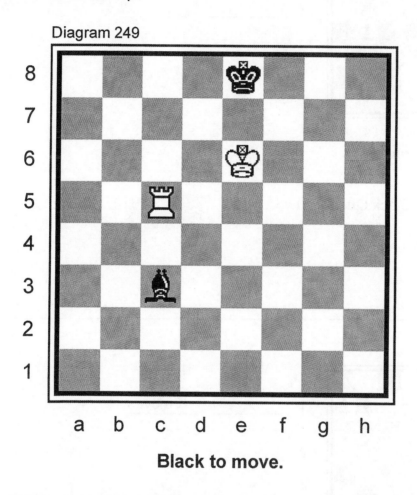

Black to move.

White just played Rc5, threatening checkmate (Rc8#), and attacking the Bishop (Rxc3) at the same time! Black cannot defend against the Double Threat, so Black moves the King to avoid checkmate and gives up the Bishop.

Circle the square where White threatens checkmate.

9 Double Threats instruction

Diagram 250

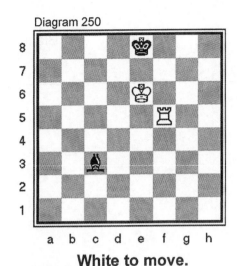

White to move.

	White	Black		White	Black
1.	Rc5	Ba1??	1.	Rc5	K moves
2.	Rc8 #		2.	Rxc3	

This one is done for you.

 To Do Checkmate or win the Black Bishop in two moves.

 How White plays Rc5, threatening to checkmate (Rc8#) and to take the Black Bishop (Rxc3). Black must move the King, and White then plays (Rxc3), winning the Black Bishop.

Diagram 251

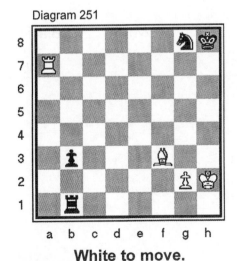

White to move.

	White	Black		White	Black
1.	_____	R moves??	1.	_____	N moves
2.	_____ #		2.	_____	

Your turn now!

 To Do Checkmate or win the Black Rook in two moves.

How White plays Be4, threatening to checkmate (Rh7#) and to take the Black Rook (Bxb1). Black must move the Knight to avoid mate. Then, White plays Bxb1, winning the Black Rook.

131

9 Double Threats instruction

Diagram 252

White to move.

	White	Black		White	Black
1.	_____	Nb5??	1.	_____	f6
2.	_____ #		2.	_____	

To Do Checkmate or win the Black Knight in two moves.

How White plays Qd4, threatening to checkmate (Qg7# or Qh8#) and to take the Black Knight (Qxa7). After Black plays . . . f6, White plays Qxa7, winning the Black Knight on a7.

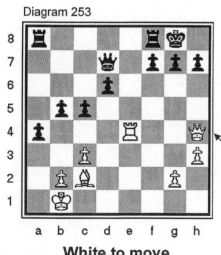

Diagram 253

Notice that when the White Rook moves, the White Bishop joins the White Queen in attacking h7.

White to move.

	White	Black		White	Black
1.	_____	Qxe7??	1.	_____	g6/h6
2.	_____ #		2.	_____	

To Do Checkmate or win the Black Queen in two moves.

How White plays Re7, threatening to checkmate (Qxh7#) and to take the Black Queen (Rxd7). Black plays . . . g6 or . . . h6 to avoid mate. Then, White plays Rxd7, winning the Black Queen.

132

9 Double Threats

Diagram 254

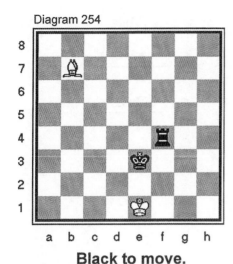

Black to move.

	White	Black		White	Black
1.	• • •	_____	1.	• • •	_____
2.	Ba8??	_____ #	2.	K moves	_____

To Do Checkmate or win the White Bishop in two moves.

Hint Use a Rook move that threatens checkmate by the Rook and attacks the White Bishop.

Diagram 255

White to move.

	White	Black		White	Black
1.	_____	Qxc7??	1.	_____	h6
2.	_____ #		2.	_____	

To Do Checkmate or win the Black Queen in two moves.

Hint Use a Bishop move that threatens checkmate by the Rook and attacks the Black Queen.

9 Double Threats

Diagram 256

Black to move.

	White	Black		White	Black
1.	• • •		1.	• • •	
2.	Qxe1??	#	2.	Qxf2	

To Do Checkmate or win the White Queen for a Rook in two moves.

Hint Use a Rook move that threatens checkmate by the Black Rook (. . . Rh2#) and attacks the White Queen.

Diagram 257

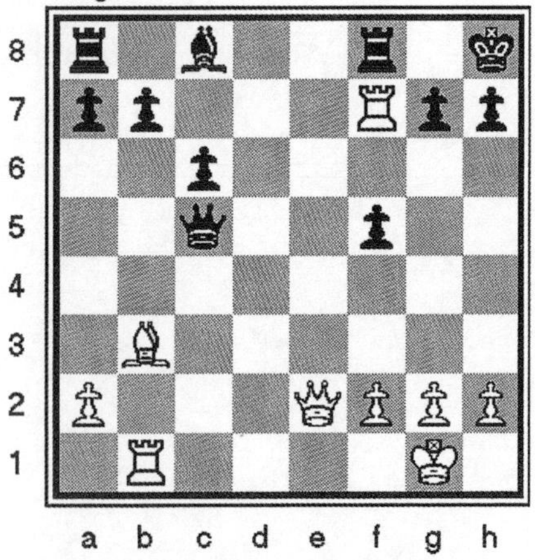

White to move.

	White	Black		White	Black
1.		Qxe5??	1.		Rxf7
2.	#		2.		

To Do Checkmate or win the Black Queen for a Rook in two moves.

Hint Use a Queen move that threatens checkmate by the White Queen (Qxg7#) and attacks the Black Queen.

134

9 Double Threats

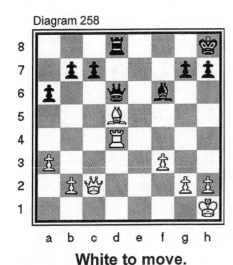

Diagram 258

White to move.

	White	Black		White	Black
1.	_____	Qxd4??	1.	_____	Kxg8
2.	_____ #		2.	_____	

To Do Checkmate or win the Black Queen for a Bishop and Rook in two moves.

Hint Use a Bishop move that threatens checkmate by the White Queen. The Bishop move also uncovers an attack against the Black Queen by the White Rook.

Diagram 259

White to move.

	White	Black		White	Black
1.	_____	Nxf5??	1.	_____	f6
2.	_____ #		2.	_____	

Do you see why Nc6 does not work as White's move? (Black can play Qxe3+)

To Do Checkmate or win the Black Queen for a Knight in two moves.

Hint Use a Knight move that threatens checkmate by the White Queen and attacks the Black Queen.

135

9 Double Threats

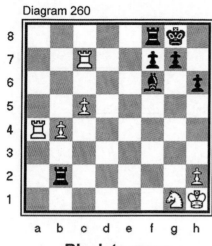

Diagram 260

Black to move.

	White	Black		White	Black
1.	• • •		1.	• • •	
2.	Rd7??	#	2.	N moves	

To Do Checkmate or win the White Rook on c7 in two moves.

Hint Use a Bishop move that threatens checkmate by the Black Rook (. . . Rxh2) and attacks the White Rook on c7.

Diagram 261

Black to move.

	White	Black		White	Black
1.	• • •		1.	• • •	
2.	Rxd4??	#	2.	Nf2	

To Do Checkmate or win the White Rook on h4 in two moves.

Hint Use a Queen move that threatens checkmate and attacks the White Rook on h4.

136

9 Double Threats

Diagram 262

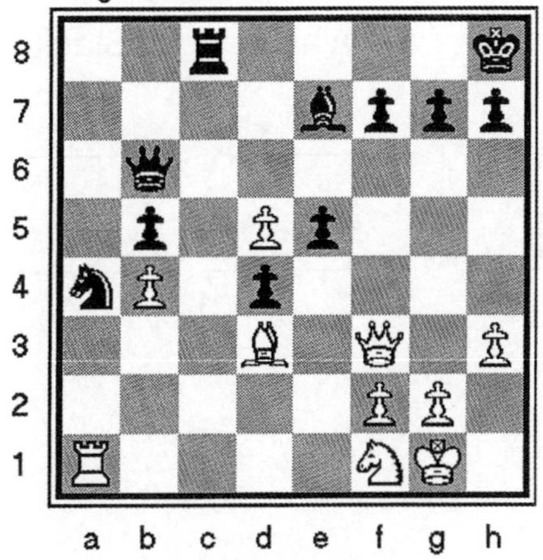

White to move.

White	Black	White	Black
1. _____	R moves??	1. _____	g6
2. _____ #		2. _____ +	

To Do   Checkmate or win the Black Rook in two moves.

Hint   Use a Queen move that threatens checkmate and attacks the Black Rook.

Diagram 263

White to move.

White	Black	White	Black
1. _____	g6??	1. _____	Kf8
2. _____ +	_____	2. _____ +	
3. _____ #			

To Do   Checkmate in three moves or win the Black Rook in two moves.

Hint   Use a Queen move that threatens checkmate and attacks the Black Rook.

9 Double Threats

Diagram 264

Black to move.

	White	Black		White	Black
1.	• • •		1.	• • •	
2.	Ra6??	#	2.	Bf5	

To Do Checkmate or win the White Rook on a3 in two moves.

Hint Use a Queen move that threatens checkmate and attacks the White Rook on a3.

Diagram 265

Black to move.

	White	Black		White	Black
1.	• • •	+	1.	• • •	+
2.	g3		2.	g3	
3.	Ra6??	#	3.	Bf5	

To Do Checkmate or win the White Rook on a3 in three moves.

Hint Use a Queen check (. . . Qc7+). Follow this with another Queen move, a move that threatens checkmate and attacks the White Rook on a3.

9 Double Threats

Diagram 266

White to move.

	White	Black		White	Black
1.	_____	Nxf5??	1.	_____	Bg7
2.	___#___		2.	_____	

To Do Checkmate or win the Black Rook for a Knight in two moves.

Hint Use a Knight move that threatens checkmate from the White Rook. The Knight move also uncovers an attack on the Black Rook by the White Bishop.

Diagram 267

White to move.

	White	Black		White	Black
1.	_____	Rc3??	1.	_____	Bf5
2.	___#___		2.	_____	

To Do Checkmate or win the Black Rook on c6 in two moves.

Hint Use a Queen move that threatens checkmate by the Queen and attacks the Black Rook on c6.

9 Double Threats

Diagram 268

White to move.

	White	Black		White	Black
1.	_____	Red8??	1.	_____	f6
2.	_____ #		2.	_____	

To Do Checkmate or win the Black Rook on d6 in two moves.

Hint Use a Queen move that threatens checkmate by the Queen and attacks the Black Rook on d6.

Diagram 269

White to move.

	White	Black		White	Black
1.	_____	Rxd6?	1.	_____	Rxd6?
2.	_____	Red8??	2.	_____	f6
3.	_____ #		3.	_____	

To Do Checkmate or win the Black Bishop in three moves.

Hint Use a Rook sacrifice (Rxd6!). Follow this with a Queen move that threatens checkmate by the Queen and attacks the Black Rook on d6.

9 Double Threats

Diagram 270

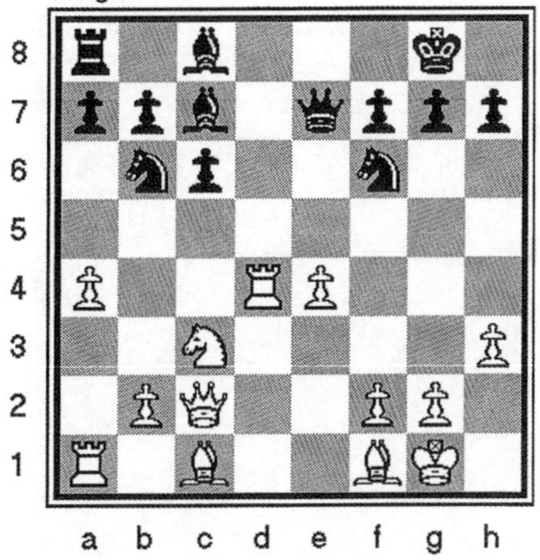

8 7 6 5 4 3 2 1
a b c d e f g h

Black to move.

	White	Black		White	Black
1.	• • •	_____	1.	• • •	_____
2.	Rd3??	_____ #	2.	g3/f4	_____

To Do Checkmate or win a White Rook in two moves.

Hint Use a Queen move that threatens checkmate and attacks the White Rook on d4.

Diagram 271

8 7 6 5 4 3 2 1
a b c d e f g h

Black to move.

	White	Black		White	Black
1.	• • •	_____	1.	• • •	_____
2.	Rxd4?	_____	2.	Rxd4?	_____
3.	Rd3??	_____ #	3.	g3/f4	_____

To Do Checkmate or win the White Knight on d4—following a Rook exchange—in three moves.

Hint Use a Rook sacrifice. Follow this with a Queen move that threatens checkmate by the Queen and attacks the Black Rook on d4.

141

9 Double Threats

Diagram 272

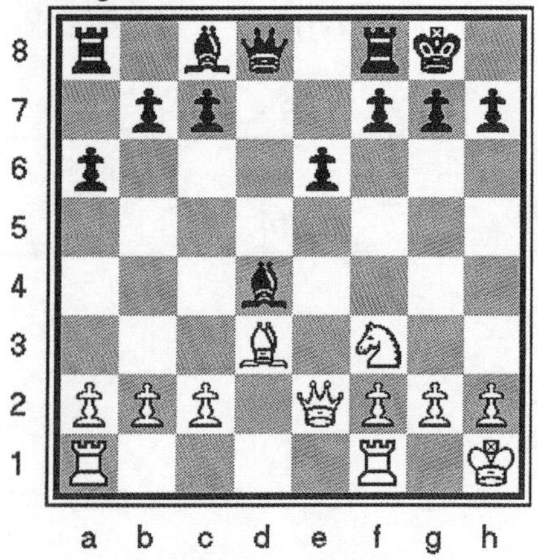

8 7 6 5 4 3 2 1

a b c d e f g h

White to move.

	White	Black		White	Black
1.	_____	c5 ??	1.	_____	f5/g6
2.	_____ #		2.	_____	

To Do Checkmate or win the Black Bishop on d4 in two moves.

Hint Use a Queen move that threatens checkmate by the Queen and attacks the Black Bishop.

Diagram 273

8 7 6 5 4 3 2 1

a b c d e f g h

White to move.

	White	Black		White	Black
1.	_____	Re8 ??	1.	_____	Qh5
2.	_____ +	Kf8	2.	_____	
3.	_____ #				

To Do Checkmate in three moves or win the Black Bishop on e7 in two moves.

Hint Use a Queen move that threatens checkmate by the Queen and attacks the Black Bishop.

142

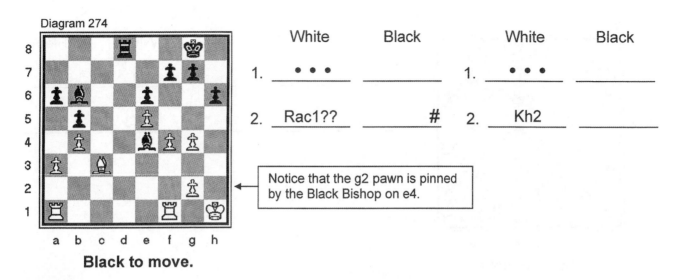

Diagram 274

Black to move.

	White	Black		White	Black
1.	• • •	_____	1.	• • •	_____
2.	Rac1??	_____ #	2.	Kh2	_____

Notice that the g2 pawn is pinned by the Black Bishop on e4.

To Do Checkmate or win the White Bishop in two moves.

Hint Use a Rook move that threatens checkmate by the Rook and attacks the White Bishop.

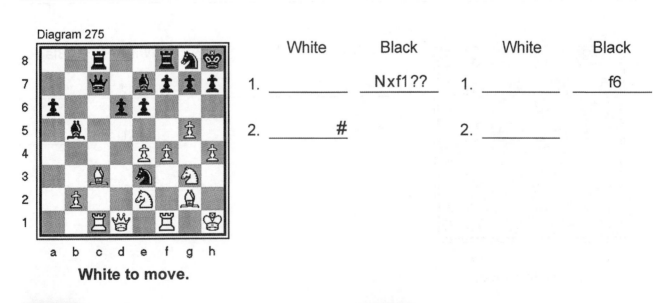

Diagram 275

White to move.

	White	Black		White	Black
1.	_____	Nxf1??	1.	_____	f6
2.	_____ #		2.	_____	

To Do Checkmate or win the Black Knight on e3 in two moves.

Hint Use a Queen move that threatens checkmate by the Queen and attacks the Black Knight.

Diagram 276

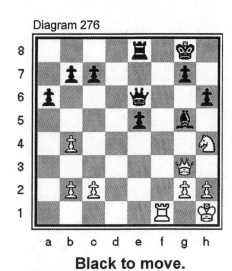

Black to move.

	White	Black		White	Black
1.	• • •	_____	1.	• • •	_____
2.	Nf3??	_____ +	2.	Qf3	_____

To Do Win the White Rook or Knight in two moves.

Hint Use a Queen move that attacks the White Rook and Knight.

Diagram 277

Black to move.

	White	Black		White	Black
1.	• • •	_____	1.	• • •	_____
2.	Rxe3??	_____ #	2.	Qd1	_____

To Do Checkmate or win the White Knight in two moves.

Hint Use a Queen move that threatens checkmate by the Rook (if White plays Rook takes Queen), and attacks the White Knight.

9 Double Threats

Diagram 278

Black to move.

	White	Black		White	Black
1.	• • •	_____	1.	• • •	_____
2.	Qxa7??	_____ #	2.	Qxe4	_____

To Do Checkmate or win the White Queen for a Bishop in two moves.

Hint Use a Bishop move that both threatens checkmate by the Knight on g5 (. . . Nh3#) and attacks the White Queen.

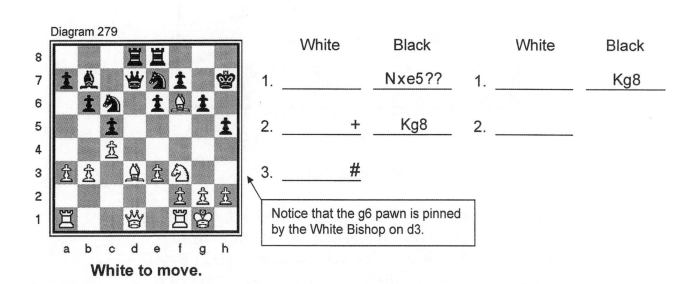

Diagram 279

White to move.

	White	Black		White	Black
1.	_____	Nxe5??	1.	_____	Kg8
2.	_____ +	Kg8	2.	_____	
3.	_____ #				

Notice that the g6 pawn is pinned by the White Bishop on d3.

To Do Checkmate in three moves or win the Black Queen for a Knight in two moves.

Hint Use a Knight move that both threatens checkmate by the White Queen in two moves and attacks the Black Queen.

145

10 Promoting Pawns introduction

Promoting a pawn, often called *Queening a Pawn*, is one of the most powerful moves in chess. Promoting a pawn often results in being a Queen ahead! Because of this, sacrificing one or more pieces to make it possible to promote a pawn may be the best strategy you have. Promoting a pawn often takes two or more moves to set up, as shown in Diagram 280.

Diagram 280

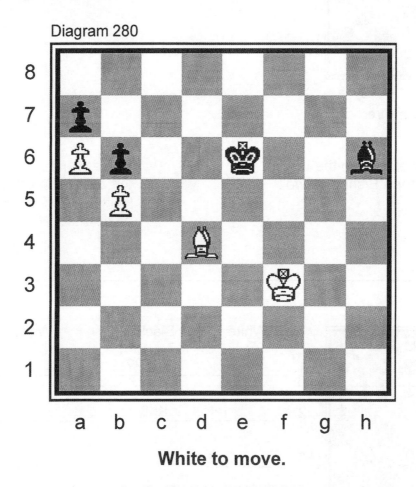

White to move.

White can sacrifice the Bishop (Bxb6!) and create a passed pawn on a6 that Black cannot stop from becoming a Queen. After White plays Bxb6!, Black plays . . . axb6. White then plays a7 and cannot be stopped on the next move from playing a8 = Q!

Circle the White Pawn that will become a Queen.

10 Promoting Pawns instruction

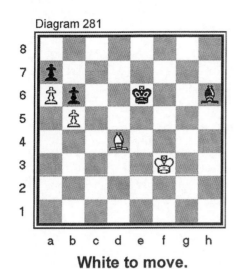

Diagram 281

White to move.

	White	Black
1.	Bxb6	axb6
2.	a7!	K/B moves
3.	a8 = Q	

This one is done for you.

To Do Promote the a-pawn to a Queen in three moves.

How White plays Bxb6!, sacrificing the Bishop. When Black plays axb6, White reponds a7! Whatever move Black makes, White plays a8 = Q, promoting the a-pawn to a Queen.

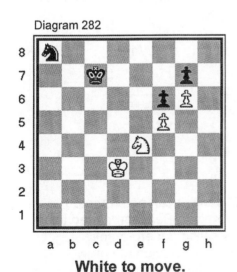

Diagram 282

White to move.

	White	Black
1.	_____	gxf6
2.	_____	K/N moves
3.	____ = Q	

Your turn now!

To Do Promote the g-pawn to a Queen in three moves.

How White plays Nxf6, sacrificing a Knight for a pawn. After Black plays . . . gxf6, White plays g7! Whatever move Black makes, White plays g8 = Q, promoting the g-pawn to a Queen.

147

10 Promoting Pawns instruction

Diagram 283

White to move.

	White	Black
1.	_____	a x b6
2.	_____	Any move
3.	_____ = Q	

To Do Promote the a-pawn to a Queen in three moves.

How White plays Q x b6!, winning a Rook or creating a passed a-pawn that Black cannot stop. When Black plays . . . a x b6, White plays a7, followed by a8 = Q!.

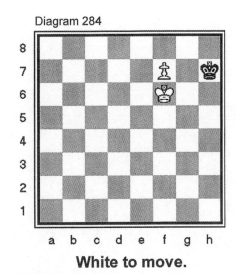

Diagram 284

White to move.

	White	Black			White	Black
1.	_____	Kh6		1.	_____ ??	
					stalement	
2.	_____ #					

Underpromotion

When a pawn reaches the 8th rank, it can be promoted to a Queen, Rook, Bishop, or Knight. Being promoted to a piece other than a Queen is called underpromotion. Underpromotion is used to prevent a stalemate draw or to gain an advantage in a continuing game.

To Do Avoid a stalemate draw, and checkmate in two moves.

How White plays f8 = R!, avoiding f8 = Q??—a stalemate draw. After White plays f8 = R!, Black is forced to play . . . Kh6, and White checkmates Black on White's next move (Rh8#).

10 Promoting Pawns

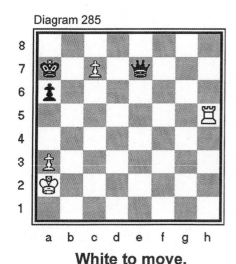

Diagram 285

White to move.

	White	Black
1.	_____ +	K moves
2.	_____	

To Do Win the Black Queen and end up a Knight and Rook ahead in two moves.

Hint Underpromote the c-pawn, forking the Black King and Queen. This underpromation wins the Black Queen as a result.

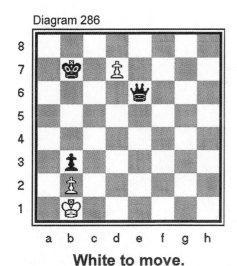

Diagram 286

White to move.

	White	Black
1.	_____ +	K moves
2.	_____	

To Do Win the Black Queen and end up a Knight ahead in two moves.

Hint Underpromote the d-pawn, forking the Black King and Queen. This underpromotion wins the Black Queen as a result.

10 Promoting Pawns

Diagram 287

Black to move.

	White	Black
1.	• • •	
2.	hxg3	
3.	Any move	= Q

To Do Promote the h-pawn to a Queen in three moves.

Hint Start with a Bishop sacrifice. Follow this by pushing the passed h-pawn.

Diagram 288

Black to move.

	White	Black
1.	• • •	
2.	bxa4	
3.	axb3	
4.	Any move	= Q

To Do Promote the a-pawn to a Queen in four moves.

Hint Begin with a Bishop sacrifice (. . . Ba4!). Next, use a pawn sacrifice (. . . b3!). Finally, push the passed a-pawn.

10 Promoting Pawns

Diagram 289

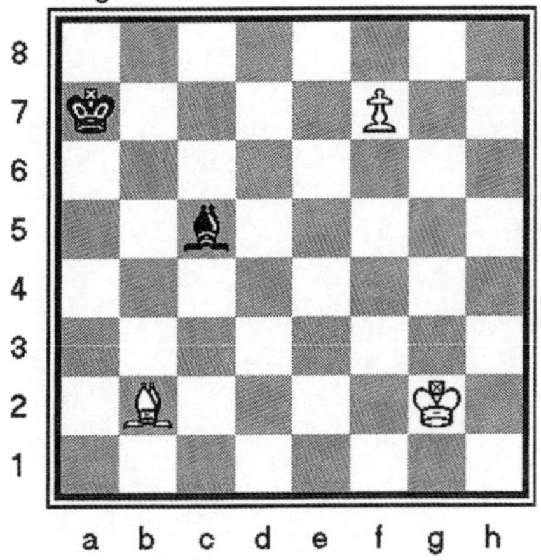

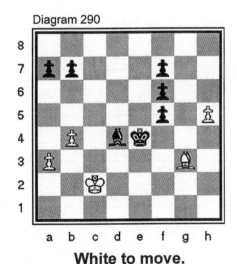

White to move.

	White	Black		White	Black
1.	_____	Bxd4	1.	_____	Kb6?
2.	_____ =Q		2.	_____ +	Kxc5
			3.	_____ =Q+	

To Do Promote the f-pawn to a Queen in two or three moves.

Hint Use a Bishop sacrifice. Make a Bishop move that pins the Black Bishop to its King, allowing the f-pawn to Queen safely!

Diagram 290

White to move.

	White	Black
1.	_____	Kxf4
2.	_____	Any move
3.	_____	Any move
4.	_____ =Q	

To Do Promote the h-pawn to a Queen in four moves.

Hint Use a Bishop sacrifice. Follow this by pushing the h-pawn. Notice that the Bishop sacrifice blocks the Black Bishop and the Black pawns on the f file. Black cannont stop the White h-pawn.

Diagram 291

8 7 6 5 4 3 2 1
a b c d e f g h

White to move.

	White	Black
1.		Nxg7
2.		N moves
3.		Any move
4.		= Q

To Do Promote the h-pawn to a Queen in four moves.

Hint Use a Knight sacrifice (Nxg7!). Follow this by pushing the h-pawn, a pawn that Black cannot stop.

Diagram 292

8 7 6 5 4 3 2 1
a b c d e f g h

Black to move.

	White	Black		White	Black
1.	• • •		1.	• • •	
2.	Rxe1		2.	Ne2?	
3.	Kxe1		3.	Nxg1	
4.	Any move	= Q	4.	Any move	= Q

To Do Promote the h-pawn to a Queen in four moves.

Hint Use a Rook trade (. . . Re1!). Follow this by a Knight sacrifice. Then, push the h-pawn to the queening square.

10 Promoting Pawns

Diagram 293

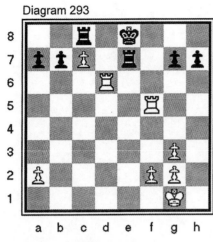

White to move.

	White		Black		White		Black
1.	_____	+	Rxd8	1.	_____	+	Rxd8
2.	_____	+	Kxf8	2.	_____	+	Kd7??
3.	_____	= Q+		3.	_____	= Q+	

 To Do Promote the c-pawn to a Queen in three moves.

Hint Use a Rook check, protected by the c-pawn. Follow this by a Rook sacrifice check (Rf8+). Then, promote the c-pawn.

Diagram 294

White to move.

	White		Black
1.	_____	+	Rxd6
2.	_____	= Q	

 To Do Promote the b7 pawn to a Queen in two moves.

Hint Use a Rook sacrifice check. Then, push the b7 pawn. This check forces the Black Rook to capture (or be captured!), allowing the b7 pawn to promote to a Queen.

10 Promoting Pawns

Diagram 295

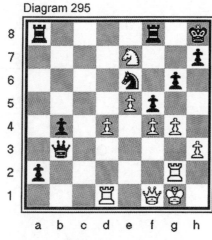

Black to move.

	White	Black
1.	• • •	
2.	Q x d1	= Q

To Do Promote the a-pawn to a Queen in two moves.

Hint Start with a Queen sacrifice (. . . Q x d1). Follow this by promoting the a-pawn to a Queen.

Diagram 296

Black to move.

	White	Black
1.	• • •	+
2.	Q x f1	+
3.	Q x e1	= Q+

To Do Promote the f-pawn to a Queen in three moves.

Hint Start with a Queen sacrifice check (. . . Q x f1+). Follow this with a Rook check. Then, recapture to promote the f-pawn to a Queen.

10 Promoting Pawns

Diagram 297

White to move.

	White	Black
1.	_____	cxd5
2.	_____	Any move
3.	_____	Any move
4.	_____ = Q	

To Do Promote the a-pawn to a Queen in four moves.

Hint Start with a Queen sacrifice. This sacrifice makes it possible to promote the a-pawn to a Queen.

Diagram 298

White to move.

	White	Black		White	Black
1.	_____ +	Qxd6	1.	_____ +	Qxd6
2.	_____	Any move	2.	_____	Qxc7?
3.	_____ = Q		3.	_____	

To Do Promote the c-pawn to a Queen, or (after a Queen trade) end up a Rook ahead in three moves.

Hint Start with a Queen sacrifice check (Qxd6+). Then, either promote the c-pawn to a Queen or capture the Black Queen after it is sacrificed to stop the advancing pawn.

155

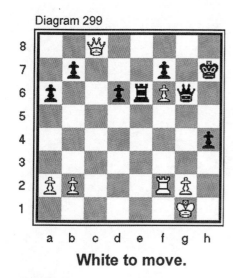

Diagram 299

White to move.

	White	Black
1.	_____	fxe6
2.	_____	Qg7
3.	_____ = Q	

To Do Promote the f-pawn to a Queen in three moves.

Hint Start with a Queen sacrifice (Qxe6!). This sacrifice makes it possible to promote the f-pawn to a Queen.

Diagram 300

White to move.

	White	Black
1.	_____ +	Kh7
2.	_____	fxe6
3.	_____	Qg7
4.	_____ = Q	

To Do Promote the f-pawn to a Queen in four moves.

Hint Start with a Queen check. Follow the check with a Queen sacrifice (Qxe6!). This sacrifice makes it possible to promote the f-pawn to a Queen.

10 Promoting Pawns

Diagram 301

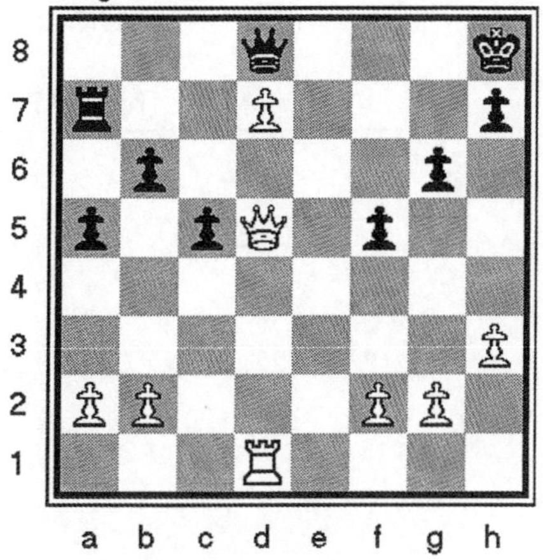

	White	Black
1.	_____ +	Kg8
2.	_____ +	Qxe8
3.	_____ = Q+	

White to move.

To Do Promote the d-pawn to a Queen in three moves.

Hint Use two Queen checks, forcing a Queen trade.

Diagram 302

	White	Black
1.	_____ +	Qxe6
2.	_____	Any move
3.	_____ = Q	

White to move.

To Do Promote the e7 pawn to a Queen in three moves.

Hint Use a Queen check to force a Queen trade. Follow this by promoting the e-pawn to a Queen.

10 Promoting Pawns

Diagram 303

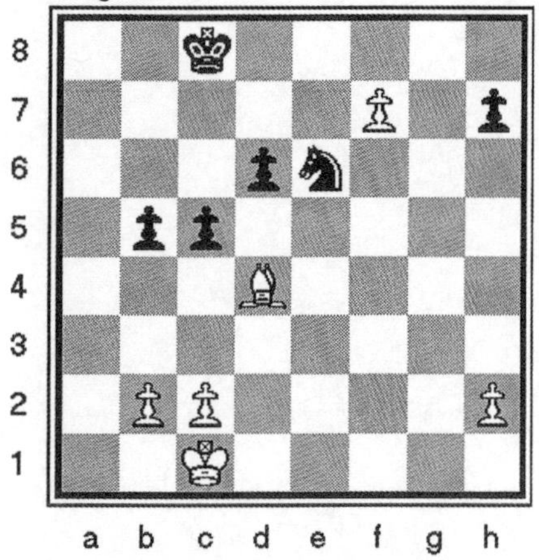

White to move.

White	Black		White	Black
1. _____	Kd7	1. _____	Nxg7??
2. ____ = Q	Nxf8	2. ____ = Q+	
3. _____			

To Do Win the Black Knight for a pawn in three moves, or promote the f-pawn to a Queen in two moves.

Hint Begin by attacking the f8 square with the Bishop. Then, promote the f-pawn to a Queen.

Diagram 304

White to move.

White	Black		White	Black
1. ____ +	Kh8	1. ____ +	Nxc4??
2. _____	g6	2. ____ #	
3. ____ = Q	Nxe8		
4. _____			

To Do Win the Black Knight for a pawn in four moves, or check-mate in two moves.

Hint Begin with a Bishop check. Follow this by attacking the e8 square with the Bishop. Then, promote the e-pawn to a Queen.

10 Promoting Pawns

Diagram 305

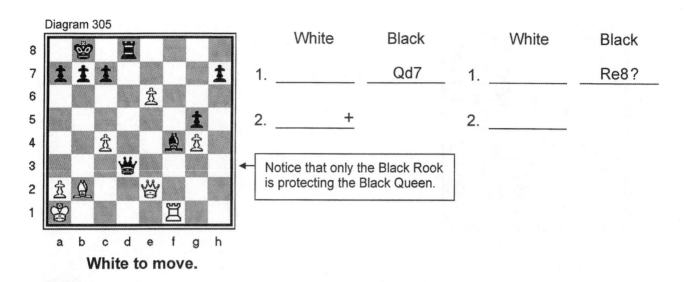

White to move.

	White	Black		White	Black
1.	_____	Qd7	1.	_____	Re8 ?
2.	_____ +		2.	_____	

 Notice that only the Black Rook is protecting the Black Queen.

To Do Win the Black Rook or Queen in two moves.

Hint Push the e-pawn, threatening the Black Rook.

Diagram 306

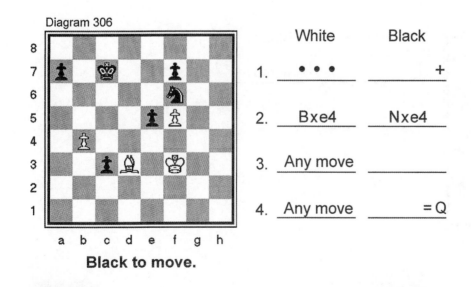

Black to move.

	White	Black
1.	• • •	_____ +
2.	Bxe4	Nxe4
3.	Any move	_____
4.	Any move	= Q

To Do Force a Bishop and Knight trade, and promote the c-pawn to a Queen in four moves.

Hint Push the e-pawn, checking the White King and forking the King and Bishop. Next, after the Bishop and Knight are traded, push the c-pawn to c8 for a Queen.

159

Diagram 307

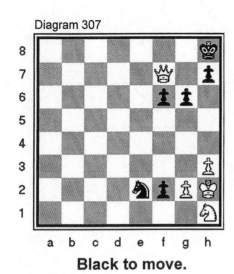

Black to move.

White	Black
1. • • •	#

To Do Checkmate in one move.

Hint Use an Underpromotion. (Promote the pawn to something other than a Queen!)

Diagram 308

White to move.

White	Black
1.	Any move
2. #	

To Do Checkmate in two moves.

Hint Use an Underpromotion. Black cannot stop White from putting a Knight on c7 and checkmating!

10 Promoting Pawns

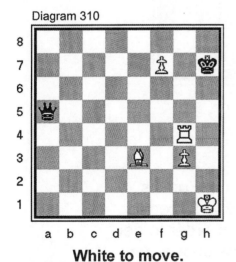

Diagram 309

White to move.

	White	Black		White	Black
1.	_____		1.	_____ ??	
				stalemate	

To Do Come out a Rook ahead and avoid a stalemate draw.

Hint Use an Underpromotion.

Diagram 310

White to move.

	White	Black
1.	_____ +	Kh8
2.	_____ +	Qe5
3.	_____ #	

To Do Checkmate in three moves.

Hint Use an Underpromotion with check, followed by a Bishop check and then checkmate.

11 Removing the Guard introduction

To **Remove the Guard** is to attack a piece that is *guarding* the opponent against checkmate, or that is guarding a piece from being captured. Sometimes Removing the Guard can be simple, as shown in Diagram 311. Other times, it takes two or three moves to set up.

Diagram 311

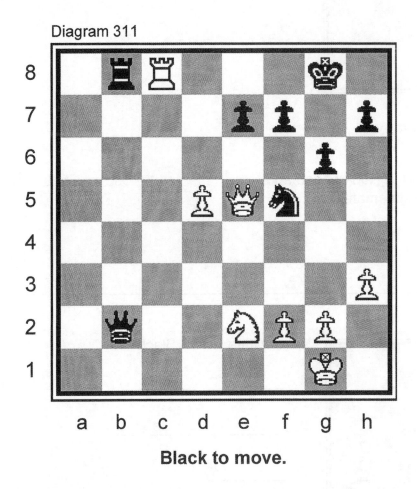

Black to move.

White has just played Rc8+. The Black Rook is guarding the Black Queen, but Black is forced to capture the White Rook (. . . Rxc8) in order to get out of check. White then captures the unguarded Black Queen (Qxb2!).

Circle the White piece that will capture Black's Queen.

162

11 Removing the Guard instruction

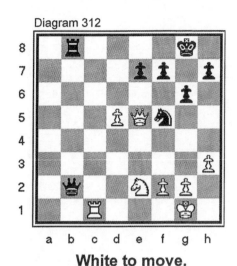

Diagram 312

White to move.

	White	Black
1.	Rc8 +	Rxc8
2.	Qxb2	

This one is done for you.

 To Do Win the Black Queen for a Rook in two moves.

 How White plays RC8+, forcing Black to play . . . Rxc8. Black's move leaves its Queen unguarded. White then plays Qxb2, winning the Black Queen for a Rook.

Diagram 313

White to move.

	White	Black
1.	_____ +	_____
2.	_____ +	Kg7
3.	_____	

Your turn now!

 To Do Win the Black Rook in three moves.

How White plays Qg4+, which forces a trade of Queens (. . . Qxg4). White then plays Rxe8+ and wins the Rook. Black is forced to play . . . Kg7. White then plays fxg4, capturing the Queen.

11 Removing the Guard instruction

Diagram 314

Black to move.

White	Black
1. • • •	+
2. _____	_____

To Do Win the White Queen for a Rook in two moves.

How Black plays . . . Rg1+, sacrificing a Rook in order to move the White King away from its Queen. White must play Kxg1. Black then plays . . . Qxe2, winning the Queen for a Rook.

Diagram 315

White to move.

White	Black
1. _____	Qxe7
2. _____ +	Any move
3. _____ +	

To Do Win both Black Rooks for a Rook in three moves.

How White plays Re7, attacking the Black Queen. Black's best move is . . . Qxe7. Black's move leaves the Black Rook on d5 unguarded. White then plays Qxd5+. After Black moves, White plays Qxa8+.

164

11 Removing the Guard

Removing the Guard

Diagram 316

8 7 6 5 4 3 2 1
a b c d e f g h

Black to move.

	White	Black		White	Black
1.	• • •	___ +	1.	• • •	___ +
2.	Kg1	___ +	2.	Re2	___

To Do Win the White Rook in two moves.

Hint Use a Bishop check to Remove the Guard (the King) from the White Rook.

Diagram 317

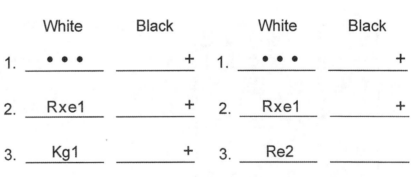

8 7 6 5 4 3 2 1
a b c d e f g h

Black to move.

	White	Black		White	Black
1.	• • •	___ +	1.	• • •	___ +
2.	Rxe1	___ +	2.	Rxe1	___ +
3.	Kg1	___ +	3.	Re2	___

To Do Win a White Rook in three moves.

Hint Begin with an exchange of Rooks on e1. Follow this with a Bishop check to Remove the Guard (the King) from the remaining White Rook.

11 Removing the Guard

Diagram 318

White to move.

	White		Black
1.	_____	+	Kxd8 _____
2.	_____		

To Do Win the Black Queen for a Rook in two moves.

Hint Use a Rook sacrifice check to Remove the Guard (the King) from the Black Queen.

Diagram 319

White to move.

	White		Black
1.	_____	+	Qxf7 _____
2.	_____	+	Kxd8 _____
3.	_____		

To Do Win the Black Queen and a pawn for a Bishop and Rook in three moves.

Hint Begin with a Bishop sacrifice check. Follow this with a Rook sacrifice check to Remove the Guard (the King) from the Black Queen.

166

11 Removing the Guard

Diagram 320

White to move.

	White	Black
1.	_____ +	K moves
2.	_____	

To Do Win the Black Knight in two moves.

Hint Use a Queen check to Remove the Guard (the King) from the Black Knight.

Diagram 321

White to move.

	White	Black
1.	_____ +	Kg7
2.	_____ +	K moves
3.	_____	

To Do Win the Black Knight in three moves.

Hint Use two Queen checks to Remove the Guard (the King) from the Black Knight.

Diagram 322

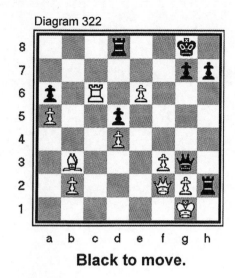

8 7 6 5 4 3 2 1

a b c d e f g h

Black to move.

	White	Black
1.	• • •	+
2.	Kxh1	

To Do Win the White Queen for a Rook in two moves.

Hint Use a Rook sacrifice check to Remove the Guard (the King) from the White Queen.

Diagram 323

8 7 6 5 4 3 2 1

a b c d e f g h

Black to move.

	White	Black
1.	• • •	+
2.	Kxc2	+

To Do Win the White Queen for a Bishop in two moves.

Hint Use a Bishop sacrifice check to Remove the Guard (the King) from the White Queen.

11 Removing the Guard

Diagram 324

White to move.

	White		Black
1.	_____	+	Kxh7
2.	_____		

To Do Win the Black Knight in two moves.

Hint Use a Rook sacrifice check to Remove the Guard (the King) from the Black Rook.

Diagram 325

White to move.

	White		Black		White		Black
1.	_____	+	Kf8	1.	_____	+	Kh6/Kh8
2.	_____			2.	_____	+	Kxh7
				3.	_____		

To Do Win the Black Knight in two or three moves.

Hint Begin with a Rook check. Follow this by winning the Knight, or by using a Rook sacrifice check to Remove the Guard (the Knight) from the Black Rook.

11 Removing the Guard

Diagram 326

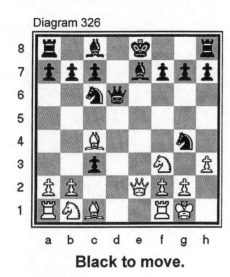

Black to move.

White	Black		White	Black
1. • • •		1.	• • •	
2. Nxd4??	#	2.	hxg4!	+

To Do Checkmate or win the Queen for two Knights in two moves.

Hint Use a Knight move to attack the White Queen or to Remove the Guard (the Knight) from the h2 square.

Diagram 327

Black to move.

White	Black		White	Black
1. • • •		1.	• • •	
2. bxc3	g5!	2.	bxc3	g5!
3. N moves		3.	B moves	

To Do Win the White Bishop or the Knight on f4 in three moves.

Hint Begin by capturing the White Knight on c3 (. . . Bxc3). Then, push the g-pawn to Remove the Guard (the remaining Knight) from the Bishop.

170

11 Removing the Guard

Diagram 328

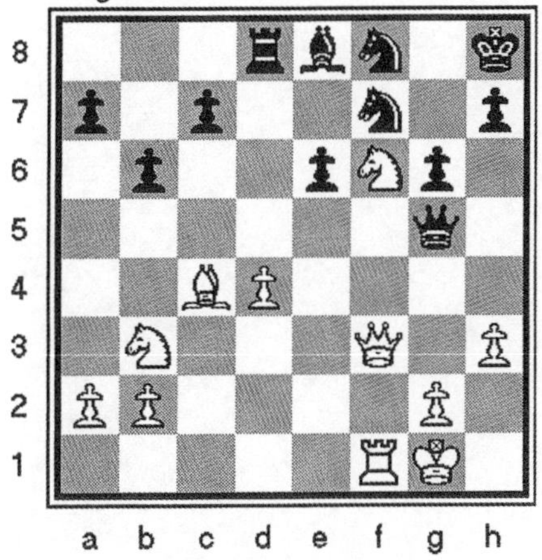

White to move.

	White	Black
1.	_____	Rxe8
2.	_____	

To Do Win the Knight on f7 in two moves.

Hint Use a Knight capture to Remove the Guard (the Bishop) from the Knight on f7.

Diagram 329

White to move.

	White	Black		White	Black
1.	_____	Bxe5	1.	_____	Rfe8
2.	_____		2.	_____	

To Do Win the Black e-pawn in two moves.

Hint Use a Knight sacrifice to Remove the Guard (the Bishop) from the Knight. If the Black Bishop takes the White Knight, the White Rook will take the Black Knight.

171

Diagram 330

White to move.

White	Black
1. _____ +	_____
2. _____	

To Do Win the Black Queen in two moves.

Hint Use a Rook check to Remove the Guard (the Bishop) from the Black Queen.

Diagram 331

Black to move.

White	Black
1. • • • _____	_____ +
2. hxg6 _____	

To Do Win the White Bishop in two moves.

Hint Use a Rook sacrifice check to Remove the Guard (the Bishop) from the White Rook.

172

11 Removing the Guard

Diagram 332

White to move.

White		Black		White		Black
1. _____	+	Rxe8		1. _____	+	Kg7
2. _____				2. _____		

To Do Win the Black Queen for a Rook in two moves.

Hint Use a Rook sacrifice check to Remove the Guard (the Rook) from the Black Queen.

Diagram 333

White to move.

White		Black		White		Black
1. _____	+	Rxf8		1. _____	+	Kh7
2. _____				2. _____		

To Do Win the Black Queen for a Rook, or win a Rook for free, in two moves.

Hint Use a Rook sacrifice check to Remove the Guard (the Rook) from the Black Queen.

Diagram 334

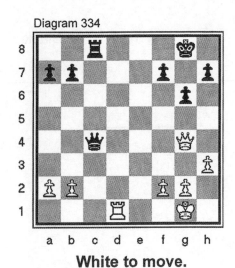

White to move.

	White	Black		White	Black
1.	_____ +	Kg7	1.	_____ +	Rxd8
2.	_____		2.	_____	

To Do Win the Black Rook, or the Queen for a Rook, in two moves.

Hint Use a Rook sacrifice check to Remove the Guard (the Rook) from the Black Queen.

Diagram 335

White to move.

	White	Black
1.	_____ +	Rxd8
2.	_____	

To Do Win the Black Queen for a Rook in two moves.

Hint Use a Rook sacrifice check to Remove the Guard (the Rook) from the Black Queen.

Diagram 336

8 · 7 · 6 · 5 · 4 · 3 · 2 · 1
a b c d e f g h

Black to move.

	White	Black		White	Black
1.		+	1.		+
2.	Rxb1		2.	Kf2??	#

To Do Win the White Queen for a Rook, or checkmate, in two moves.

Hint Use a Rook sacrifice check to Remove the Guard (the Rook) from the White Queen.

Diagram 337

8 · 7 · 6 · 5 · 4 · 3 · 2 · 1
a b c d e f g h

Black to move.

	White	Black
1.		+
2.	Rxd1	

To Do Win the White Bishop in two moves.

Hint Use a Rook sacrifice check to Remove the Guard (the Rook on c1) from the Rook on c3.

11 Removing the Guard

Diagram 338

White to move.

	White	Black		White	Black
1.	_____	Qxe8	1.	_____	Kf7
2.	___#___		2.	___#___	

To Do Checkmate on g7 or f8 in two moves.

Hint Use a Rook sacrifice to Remove the Guard (the Queen) from the g7 square.

Diagram 339

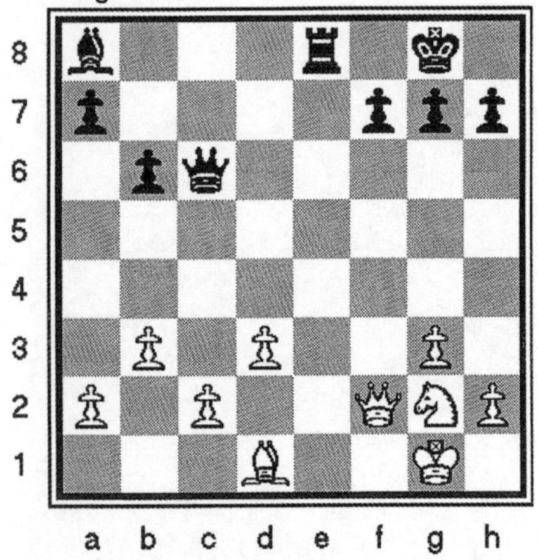

Black to move.

	White	Black		White	Black
1.	• • •	____+	1.	• • •	____+
2.	Nxe1	___#___	2.	Qxe1	___#___

To Do Checkmate on g2 or h1 in two moves.

Hint Use a Rook sacrifice check to Remove the Guard (the Queen or Knight) from the g2 square or the h1 square.

176

11 Removing the Guard

Diagram 340

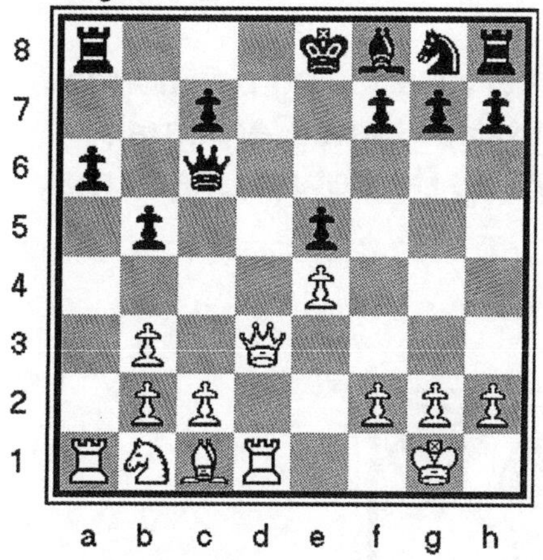

White to move.

White	Black	White	Black
1. _____	Rxa6?	1. _____	Qxa6?
2. _____ #		2. _____ #	

Black's best response to avoid checkmate is Bd6. This move, though, loses the Black Queen and the game soon after. Black's position is hopeless!

To Do Checkmate in two moves.

Hint Use a Rook sacrifice (Rxa6) to Remove the Guard (the Queen or the Rook) from the d7 square or the d8 square.

Diagram 341

White to move.

White	Black	White	Black
1. _____	Qxb8	1. _____	Rxb8
2. _____ #		2. _____ #	

To Do Checkmate in two moves.

Hint Use a Rook sacrifice to Remove the Guard (the Queen or the Rook), setting up either Nxf7# or Qg7#.

12 Perpetual Check introduction

Perpetual Check is a tactic that a player uses in an otherwise losing position to draw the game by repeatedly checking the opponent's King. Some Perpetual Checks are simple, as shown in Diagram 342. Other times, Perpetual Check may take two or more moves to set up.

Diagram 342

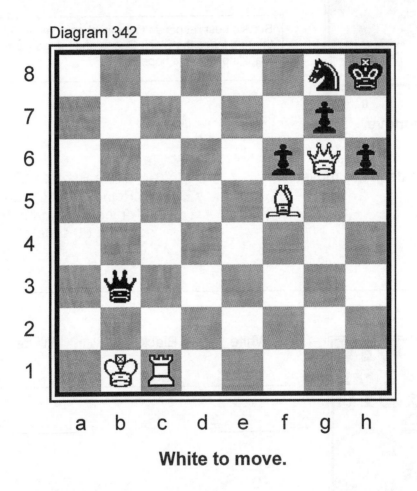

White to move.

White is threatening checkmate in one move (Qh7#), but never gets the chance! White is in check. Black draws this game by perpetually checking the White King from the b3 and a3 squares.

Circle the Black piece that gives the Perpetual Check.

12 Perpetual Check instruction

Diagram 343

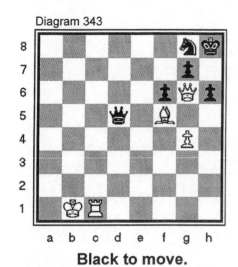

8
7
6
5
4
3
2
1

a b c d e f g h

Black to move.

	White	Black
1.	• • •	Qb3 +
2.	Ka1	Qa3 +
3.	Kb1	Qb3 +, etc.
		draw

This one is done for you.

To Do Avoid checkmate (Qh7#), and draw this otherwise losing position by using a Perpetual Check.

How Black is behind but is able to draw the game with a Perpetual Check, playing . . . Qb3+. White must play Ka1. Black then plays Qa3+, and White plays Kb1. White cannot escape check.

Diagram 344

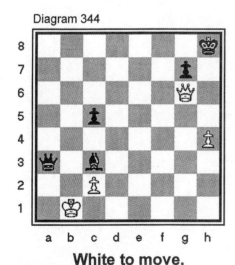

8
7
6
5
4
3
2
1

a b c d e f g h

White to move.

	White	Black		White	Black
1.	___ +	Kg8	1.	___ +	Kh7
2.	___ +		2.	___ +	
3.	___ +, etc.		3.	___ +, etc.	
	draw			draw	

Your turn now!

To Do Avoid checkmate (. . .Qa1# or . . .Qb2#), and draw this otherwise losing position by using a Perpetual Check.

How White is behind, but is able to draw the game with a Perpetual Check—alternately playing Qh5+ and Qe8+. Black is forced to play Kg8 and Kh2. Black cannot escape check. Draw!

179

12 Perpetual Check instruction

Diagram 345

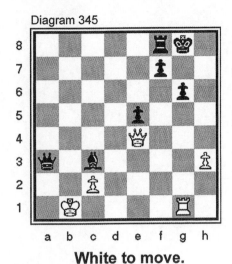

White to move.

	White	Black
1.	_____ +	fxg6 ____
2.	_____ +	_____
3.	_____ +	_____
4.	_____ +, etc.	
	draw	

To Do Avoid checkmate (. . .Qa1# or . . . Qb2#), and draw this otherwise losing position by using a Perpetual Check.

How White plays Rxg6+, sacrificing a Rook. Black plays . . . fxg6. White then plays Qxg6+, and alternately checks the Black King (Qg6+ and Qh6+). Black cannot escape check. Draw!

Diagram 346

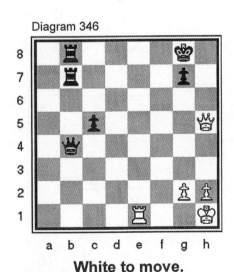

White to move.

	White	Black
1.	_____ +	_____
2.	_____ +	_____
3.	_____ +	_____
4.	_____ +, etc.	
	draw	

To Do Draw this otherwise losing position by using a Perpetual Check.

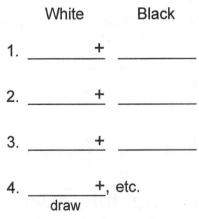

How White plays Re8+ and Black is forced to play . . . Rxe8. White next plays Qxe8+, and then alternately checks the Black King (Qe8+ and Qh5+). Black cannot escape check. Draw!

180

12 Perpetual Check

Diagram 347

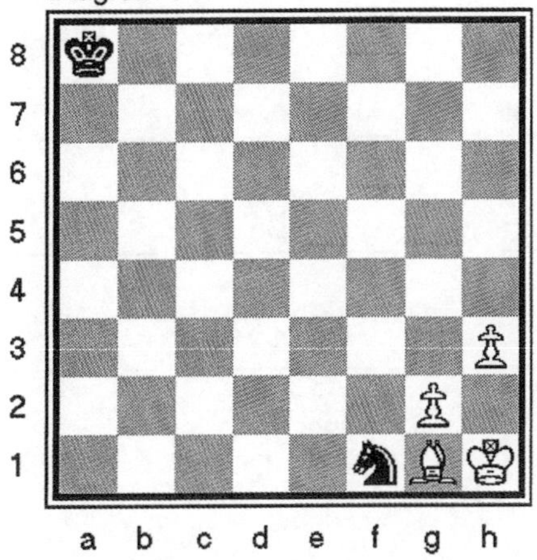

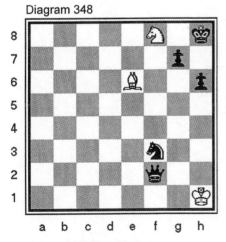

Black to move.

	White	Black
1.	• • •	+
2.	Kh2	+
3.	Kh1	+, etc.
		draw

To Do Draw this otherwise losing position by using a Perpetual Check.

Hint Use a Perpetual Check from the Black Knight.

Diagram 348

White to move.

	White	Black
1.	+	Kh7
2.	+	Kh8
3.	+, etc.	
	draw	

To Do Avoid checkmate and draw this otherwise losing position by using a Perpetual Check.

Hint Use a Perpetual Check from the White Knight.

181

12 Perpetual Check

Diagram 349

Black to move.

White	Black		White	Black
1. • • •	+	1.	• • •	+
2. Kd1	+	2.	Kb1	+
3. Kc1	+	3.	Ka1??	#
	draw			

To Do Avoid checkmate (Qg7#), and draw this otherwise losing position by using a Perpetual Check, or checkmate in three moves!.

Hint Use a Perpetual Check from the Black Knight.

Diagram 350

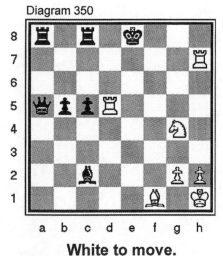

White to move.

White	Black
1. ___ +	Kf8
2. ___ +	Ke8/g8
3. ___ +	Kf8
4. ___ +, etc.	
draw	

To Do Draw this otherwise losing position by using a Perpetual Check.

Hint Use a Perpetual Check from the White Knight.

182

12 Perpetual Check

Diagram 351

Black to move.

	White	Black			White	Black	
1.	• • •		+	1.	• • •		+
2.	Kh1/h3		+	2.	Kh1		+
3.	Kh2		+	3.	Kg1		+
4.	Kh1/h3		+	4.	Kh1		+
		draw				draw	

To Do Draw this otherwise losing position by using a Perpetual Check.

Hint Use a Perpetual Check from the Black Knight. Notice that the Black Bishop attacks g1 and delivers a Discovered Check as part of the Perpetual Check.

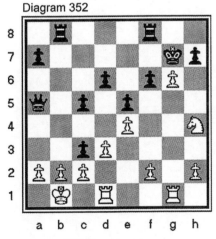

Diagram 352

White to move.

	White	Black		White	Black
1.	+	Kg8	1.	+	Kh8??
2.	+	Kg7	2.	+	Kg8
3.	+	Kg8	3.	#	
4.	+, etc.				
	draw				

To Do Draw this otherwise losing position by using a Perpetual Check, or checkmate in three moves!

Hint Use a Perpetual Check from the White Knight.

12 Perpetual Check

Diagram 353

White to move.

	White	Black		White	Black
1.	_____ +	Kg8	1.	Bf5/e4+?	Qh6!
					Blocks the check!
2.	_____ +	Kh8			
3.	_____ +, etc.				
	draw				

To Do Draw this otherwise losing position by using a Perpetual Check.

Hint Use a Perpetual Check from the White Bishop and Rook.

Diagram 354

White to move.

	White	Black
1.	_____ +	Kh7
2.	_____ +	Kg8
3.	_____ +, etc.	
	draw	

To Do Avoid checkmate and draw this otherwise losing position by using a Perpetual Check.

Hint Use a Perpetual Check from White's White Bishop.

184

12 Perpetual Check

Diagram 355

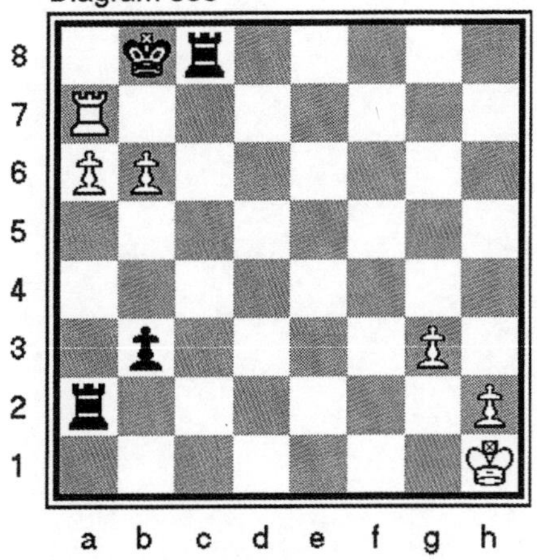

White to move.

	White		Black
1.	_____	+	Ka8
2.	_____	+	Kb8
3.	_____	+, etc.	
	draw		

To Do Avoid checkmate (. . . Rc1#) and draw this otherwise losing position by using a Perpetual Check.

Hint Use a Perpetual Check from the White Rook.

Diagram 356

Black to move.

	White	Black
1.	• • •	+
2.	Kh3	+
3.	Kh2	+
4.	Kh1	+, etc.
		draw

To Do Draw this otherwise losing position by using a Perpetual Check.

Hint Use a Perpetual Check from the Black Rook.

12 Perpetual Check

Perpetual Check

Diagram 357

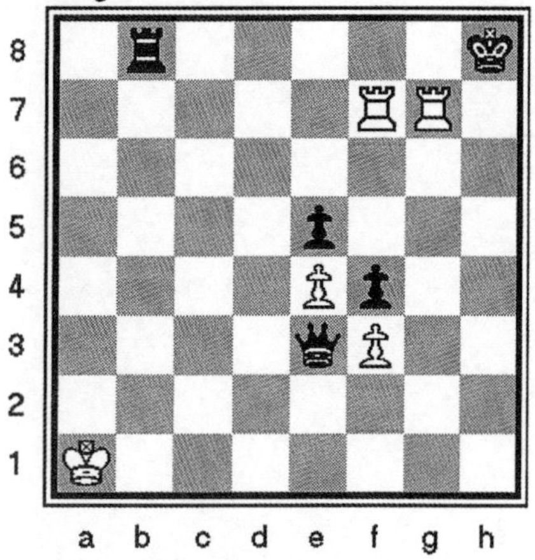

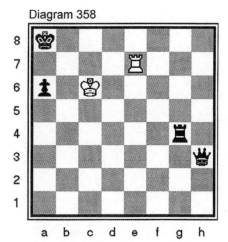

White to move.

	White		Black
1.	_____	+	Kg8
2.	Rhg7	+	Kh8
3.	_____	+, etc.	
	draw		

White to move.

To Do Avoid checkmate (... Qa3#) and draw this otherwise losing position by using a Perpetual Check.

Hint Use a Perpetual Check from a White Rook.

Diagram 358

White to move.

	White		Black
1.	_____	+	Ka7
2.	_____	+	Ka8/b8
3.	_____	+, etc.	
	draw		

White to move.

To Do Draw this otherwise losing position by using a Perpetual Check.

Hint Use a Perpetual Check from the White Rook.

186

12 Perpetual Check

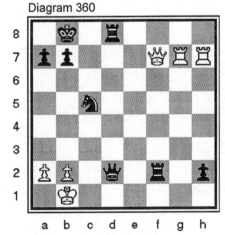

Diagram 359

White to move.

	White		Black
1.	_____	+	Ka7/b7
2.	_____	+	Ka8/b8
3.	_____	+, etc.
	draw		

To Do Draw this otherwise losing position by using a Perpetual Check.

Hint Use a Perpetual Check from the White Rook.

Diagram 360

White to move.

	White		Black		White		Black
1.	_____	+	Nxb7	1.	_____	+	Nxb7
2.	_____	+	Ka8	2.	_____	+	Kc8??
3.	_____	+	Kb8	3.	_____	#	
4.	_____	+, etc.					
	draw						

To Do Draw this otherwise losing position by using a Perpetual Check, or checkmate in three moves.

Hint Begin with a Queen sacrifice check. Follow this with a Perpetual Check from a White Rook.

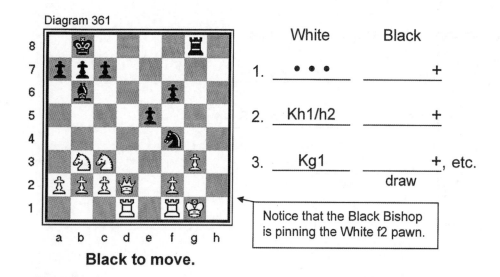

Diagram 361

Black to move.

	White	Black
1.	• • •	_____ +
2.	Kh1/h2	_____ +
3.	Kg1	_____ +, etc.
		draw

Notice that the Black Bishop is pinning the White f2 pawn.

To Do Avoid checkmate (Qd8+ and Rxd8#) and draw this otherwise losing position by using a Perpetual Check.

Hint Use a Perpetual Check from the Black Rook.

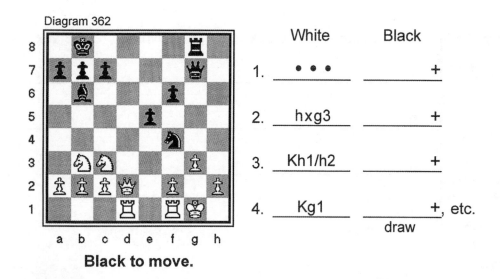

Diagram 362

Black to move.

	White	Black
1.	• • •	_____ +
2.	hxg3	_____ +
3.	Kh1/h2	_____ +
4.	Kg1	_____ +, etc.
		draw

To Do Avoid checkmate (Qd8+ and Rxd8#) and draw this otherwise losing position by using a Perpetual Check.

Hint Begin with a Queen sacrifice check. Next, use a Perpetual Check from the Black Rook.

12 Perpetual Check

Diagram 363

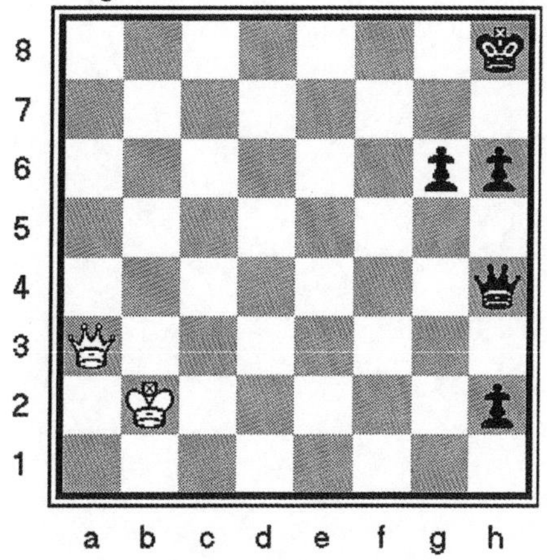

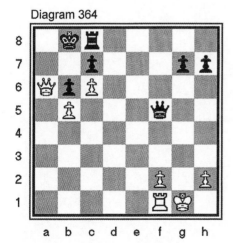

White to move.

	White		Black
1.	_____	+	Kh7
2.	_____	+	Kh8
3.	_____	+, etc.	
	draw		

To Do Stop Black from promoting the h-pawn and draw this otherwise losing position by using a Perpetual Check.

Hint Use a Perpetual Check from the White Queen.

Diagram 364

Black to move.

	White	Black	
1.	• • •	_____	+
2.	Kh1	_____	+
3.	Kg1	_____	+, etc.
		draw	

To Do Avoid checkmate (Qb7#) and draw this otherwise losing position by using a Perpetual Check.

Hint Use a Perpetual Check from the Black Queen.

189

12 Perpetual Check

Diagram 365

White to move.

	White	Black
1.	_____ +	Kh7
2.	_____ +	Kg8
3.	_____ +, etc.	
	draw	

To Do Draw this otherwise losing position by using a Perpetual Check.

Hint Use a Perpetual Check from the White Queen.

Diagram 366

White to move.

	White	Black
1.	_____ +	Rxe8
2.	_____ +	Kh7
3.	_____ +	Kg8
4.	_____ +, etc.	
	draw	

To Do Draw this otherwise losing position by using a Perpetual Check.

Hint Begin with a Rook check. Next, use a Perpetual Check from the White Queen.

12 Perpetual Check

Diagram 367

White to move.

	White		Black
1.	_____	+	Kb5
2.	_____	+	Ka5
3.	_____	+, etc.	
	draw		

To Do Avoid checkmate (. . . Qa1/b1#) and draw this otherwise losing position by using a Perpetual Check.

Hint Use a Perpetual Check from the White Queen.

Diagram 368

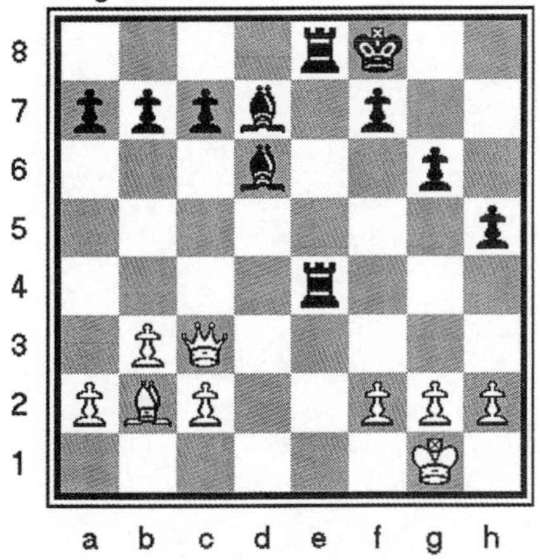

White to move.

	White		Black
1.	_____	+	Ke7
2.	_____	+	Kf8
3.	_____	+	Ke7
4.	_____	+, etc.	
	draw		

To Do Avoid checkmate (. . . Re1+ and . . . Rxe1#) and draw this otherwise losing position by using a Perpetual Check.

Hint Use a Perpetual Check from the White Queen.

191

12 Perpetual Check

Diagram 369

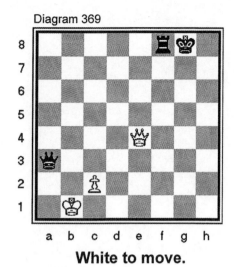

White to move.

White		Black
1. _____	+	Kh8 _____
2. _____	+	Kg8 _____
3. _____	+, etc.	
draw		

To Do Avoid being checkmated or losing the Queen (. . . Rf1+ or . . . Rb8+). Draw this otherwise losing position by using Perpetual Check.

Hint Use a Perpetual Check from the White Queen.

Diagram 370

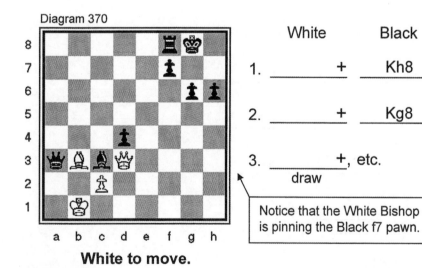

White to move.

White		Black
1. _____	+	Kh8 _____
2. _____	+	Kg8 _____
3. _____	+, etc.	
draw		

 Notice that the White Bishop is pinning the Black f7 pawn.

To Do Avoid checkmate (. . . Qa1# or . . . Qb2#) and draw this otherwise losing position by using a Perpetual Check.

Hint Use a Perpetual Check from the White Queen.

12 Perpetual Check

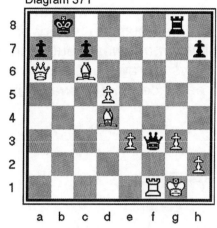

Diagram 371

	White	Black
1.	• • •	+
2.	hxg3	+
3.	Kh1	+
4.	Kg1	+, etc.
		draw

Black to move.

To Do Avoid checkmate (Qb7#) and draw this otherwise losing position by using a Perpetual Check.

Hint Begin with a Rook sacrifice check. Follow this with a Perpetual Check from the Black Queen.

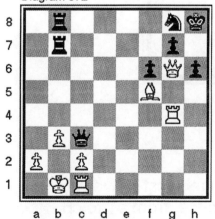

Diagram 372

	White	Black
1.	• • •	+
2.	a/cxb3	+
3.	a/cxb3	+
4.	Ka1	+, etc.
		draw

Black to move.

To Do Avoid checkmate (Qh7#) and draw this otherwise losing position by using a Perpetual Check.

Hint Begin with two Rook sacrifice checks. Follow this with a Perpetual Check from the Black Queen.

13 Zugzwang/Stalemate introduction

Zugzwang means *being required to move*, especially when you do not want to—often meaning you must make a losing move. Zugzwang can result in a victory or the win of a piece. **Stalemate** is a position where one player *must move*, but cannot make a legal move. Stalemate ends the game and is always a drawn position; neither player wins. Diagram 373 shows Black about to be placed in Zugzwang by White, with a White checkmate to follow quickly.

Diagram 373

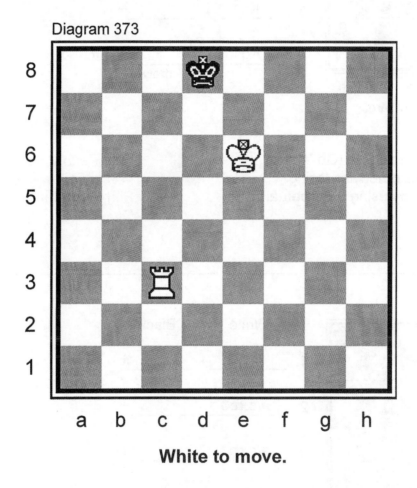

White to move.

White will checkmate Black in two moves. White's first move will be a Rook move that keeps the Rook on the c-file, from c1 to c6 (for example, Rc4). The Black King would like to stay right where it is and not move! Black is in Zugzwang. Skipping a move is not allowed! The Black King must move to e8 (. . . Ke8). White checkmates Black on the next move: Rc8#.

Circle the square where the White Rook will checkmate Black's King.

194

13 Zugzwang/Stalemate instruction

Diagram 374

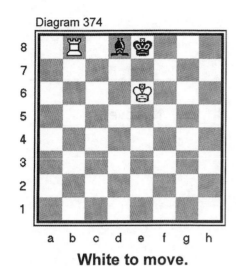

White to move.

	White	Black		White	Black
1.	Kd6	Kf7/Kf8	1.	Ra8/Rc8	Kf8
2.	Rxd8/Rxd8+		2.	Rxd8+	

This one is done for you.

To Do Win the Black Bishop in two moves.

How White moves the King (Kd6) or the Rook (Ra8/Rc8), keeping the Black Bishop pinned to its King. Black is in Zugzwang and moves . . . Kf7 or . . . Kf8, leaving the Bishop unprotected.

Diagram 375

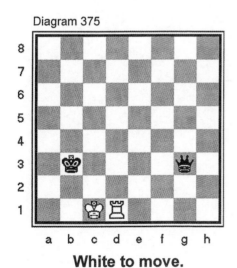

White to move.

	White	Black		White	Black
1.	_____ +	_____	1.	_____ +	Kc4??
		stalemate	2.	_____	

Your turn now!

To Do Draw this otherwise losing position in one move or win the Black Queen in two moves.

How White plays Rd3+, forcing Black to capture the Rook or lose the Queen. If Black plays . . . Qxd3, White is stalemated. If Black moves the King, White wins the Black Queen and the game.

13 Zugzwang/Stalemate instruction

Diagram 376

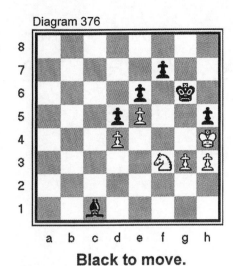

Black to move.

	White	Black		White	Black
1.	• • •		1.	• • •	
2.	g4	#	2.	N moves	#

To Do Checkmate in two moves.

How Black plays . . . Be3!, putting White in Zugzwang. White has only two possible moves, both losing! If White plays g4, Black plays . . . Bf2#. If White moves the Knight, Black plays . . . Bg5#.

Diagram 377

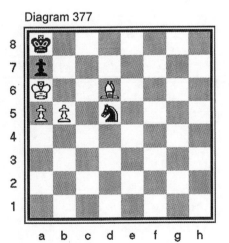

Black to move.

	White	Black
1.	• • •	+
2.	stalemate	

To Do Draw this otherwise losing position.

How Black plays . . . Nc7+!, leaving White only one move. White must take the Knight (Bxc7), forcing a stalemate draw.

13 Zugzwang/Stalemate

Diagram 378

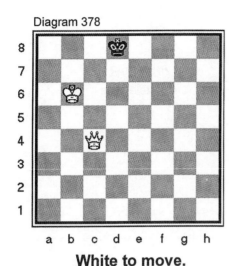

White to move.

	White	Black
1.	_____	Kc8
2.	_____ #	

To Do Checkmate in two moves.

Hint Use a Queen move to put Black into Zugzwang, forcing the Black King to move to c8 where White will checkmate it.

Diagram 379

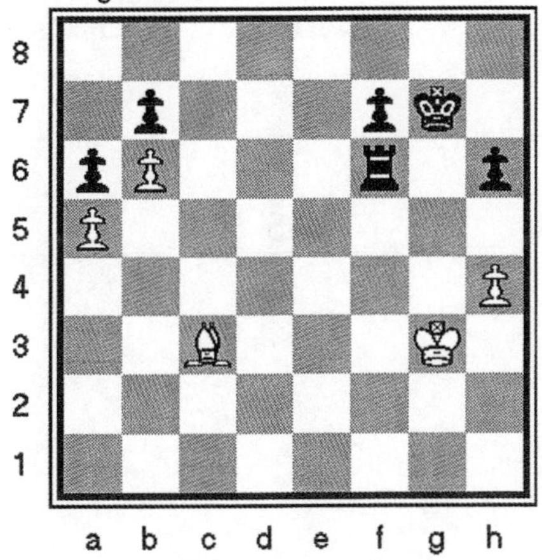

White to move.

	White	Black
1.	_____	K moves
2.	_____	

To Do Win the pinned Black Rook in two moves.

Hint Use a Pawn move to put Black into Zugzwang, forcing the Black King to leave the Black Rook unprotected.

197

Diagram 380

White to move.

	White	Black		White	Black
1.		Ka8	1.	g8 = Q/R??	
				stalemate	
2.	+	Ka7			
3.	#				

To Do Avoid a stalemate draw, and checkmate in three moves.

Hint Begin with a Pawn move to put Black in Zugzwang, forcing Black to make a King move. Now, promote the g-pawn with check, and then deliver checkmate.

Diagram 381

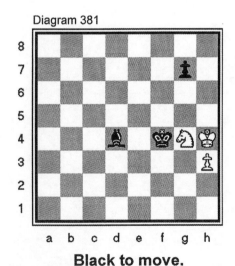

Black to move.

	White	Black		White	Black
1.	• • •		1.	• • •	
2.	Ne3	#	2.	Ne5	#

To Do Checkmate in two moves.

Hint Use a Pawn move to put White in Zugzwang, forcing White to move the Knight. Then, Black mates with the Bishop on the next move, either on f2 or f6 depending on White's move.

13 Zugzwang/Stalemate

Diagram 382

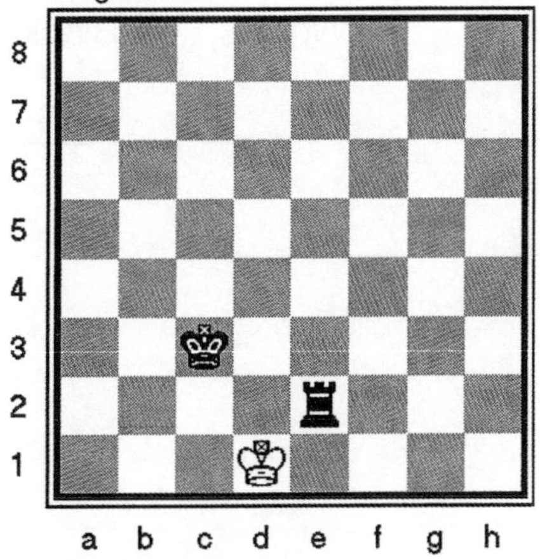

Black to move.

	White	Black
1.	• • •	______
2.	Kc1	______ #

To Do Checkmate in two moves.

Hint Use a Rook move to put White in Zugzwang, forcing the White King to move to c1.

Diagram 383

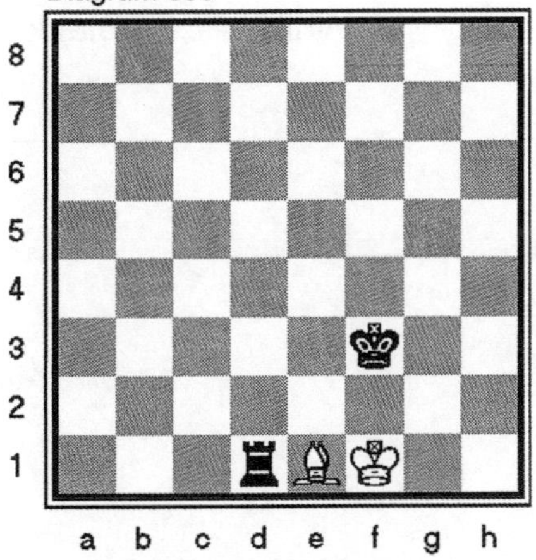

Black to move.

	White	Black		White	Black
1.	• • •	______ R move	1.	• • •	______ K move
2.	Kg1	______ +	2.	Kg1/Kg2	______

To Do Win the White Bishop in two moves.

Hint Use a Rook or King move to put White in Zugzwang, forcing the White King to leave the Bishop unprotected.

Diagram 384

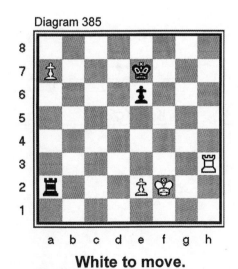

White to move.

	White	Black		White	Black
1.	_____	Rxa7	1.	_____	Kd6
2.	_____ +	K moves	2.	_____	
3.	_____				

To Do Win the Black Rook for a pawn in three moves, or promote the a-pawn in two moves.

Hint Use a Rook move to put Black in Zugzwang. If Black captures the a-pawn, White skewers the Black Rook. Black must capture the a-pawn or White will promote it to a Queen.

Diagram 385

White to move.

	White	Black		White	Black
1.	_____	Rxa7	1.	_____	Kd6
2.	_____ +	K moves	2.	_____	
3.	_____				

To Do Win the Black Rook for a pawn in three moves, or promote the a-pawn in two moves.

Hint Use a Rook move to put Black in Zugzwang. If Black captures the a-pawn, White skewers the Black Rook. If Black doesn't capture the a-pawn, White promotes it to a Queen.

13 Zugzwang/Stalemate

Diagram 386

White to move.

	White	Black		White	Black
1.	______	gxh6	1.	______	B moves
2.	______ #		2.	______ #	

To Do Checkmate in two moves.

Hint Use a Rook move to put Black in Zugzwang. Black must then capture the Rook or move the Bishop. Either way, White mates on the next move.

Diagram 387

White to move.

	White	Black		White	Black
1.	______	Qxg5	1.	______	Qg6
2.	______		2.	______	

To Do Trap the Black Queen and win it for a Rook in two moves.

Hint Use a Rook move to put Black in Zugzwang, forcing Black to make a game-losing Queen move.

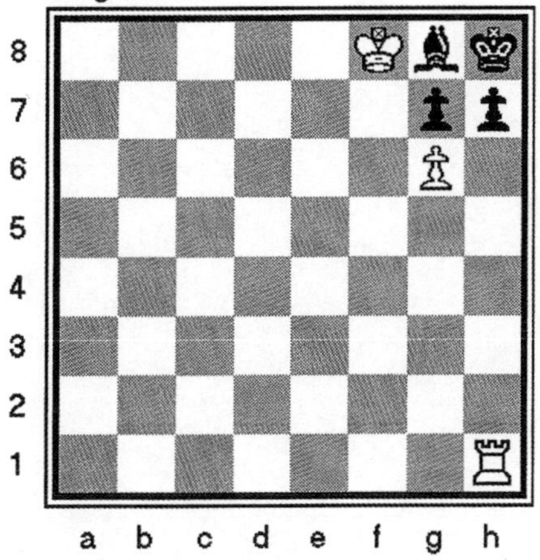

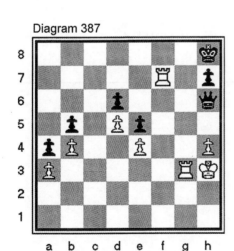

13 Zugzwang/Stalemate

Diagram 388

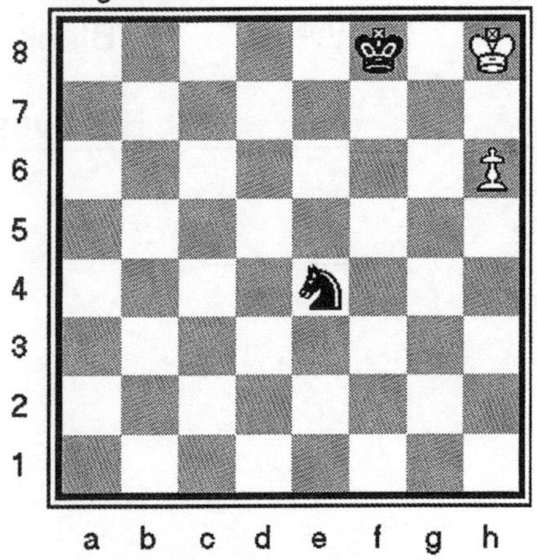

Black to move.

White	Black
1.	_____
2. h7	#

Black to move.

To Do Checkmate in two moves.

Hint Use a Knight move to put White in Zugzwang, allowing White only a pawn move. Follow this by mate with the Black Knight.

Diagram 389

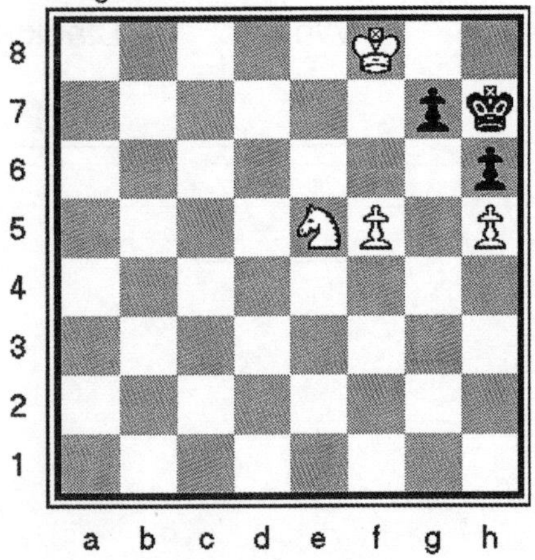

White to move.

White	Black	White	Black
1. _____	g6	1. _____	g5
2. #		2. #	

White to move.

To Do Checkmate in two moves.

Hint Use a Knight move to put Black in Zugzwang, allowing Black only a pawn move. Follow this by checkmate from the White f-pawn or h-pawn.

13 Zugzwang/Stalemate

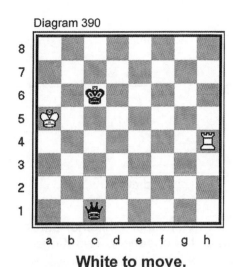

Diagram 390

8 7 6 5 4 3 2 1
a b c d e f g h

White to move.

	White	Black		White	Black
1.	_____ +	_____	1.	_____ +	Kd5??
		stalemate	2.	_____	

 To Do Draw this otherwise losing position in one move, or win the Black Queen in two moves.

 Hint Use a Rook sacrifice check to force a Stalemate draw.

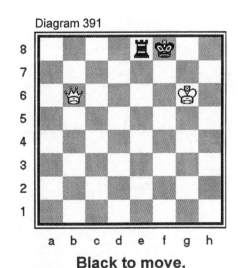

Diagram 391

8 7 6 5 4 3 2 1
a b c d e f g h

Black to move.

	White	Black		White	Black
1.	• • • _____	_____ +	1.	• • • _____	_____ +
2.	_____		2.	Kf5?? _____	_____
	stalemate				

 To Do Draw this otherwise losing position in one move, or win the White Queen in two moves.

 Hint Use a Rook sacrifice check to force a Stalemate draw.

Diagram 392

Black to move.

To Do Avoid checkmate (Qh1#) and draw this otherwise losing position by *stalemate* or by *lack of material*.

	White	Black		White	Black
1.	• • •	+	1.	• • •	+
2.		stalemate	2.	Ke4	
			3.		draw

Lack of Material Draw

A lack of material draw occurs when neither White nor Black has enough pieces to checkmate the opponent. Two Kings alone on the board is one type of a lack of material draw.

Hint Use a Rook sacrifice check. If White doesn't capture the Black Rook, Black takes the White Queen. Two Kings alone on the board is a *lack of material draw*.

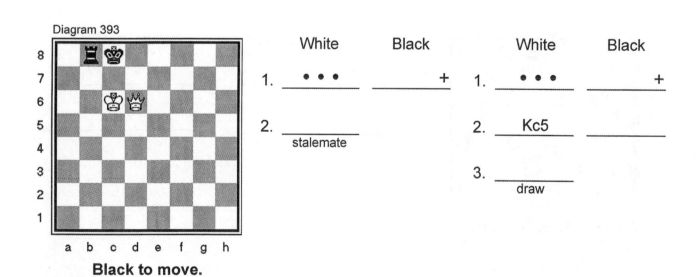

Diagram 393

Black to move.

To Do Avoid checkmate and draw this otherwise losing position by *stalemate* or by *lack of material*.

	White	Black		White	Black
1.	• • •	+	1.	• • •	+
2.		stalemate	2.	Kc5	
			3.		draw

Hint Use a Rook sacrifice check.

13 Zugzwang/Stalemate

Diagram 394

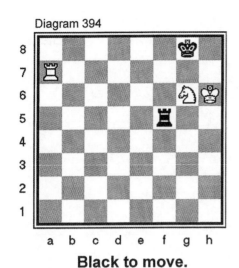

Black to move.

	White	Black
1.	• • •	_____ +
2.	_____	
	stalemate	

To Do Draw this otherwise losing position.

Hint Use a Rook sacrifice check to force Stalemate draw!

Diagram 395

Black to move.

	White	Black		White	Black
1.	• • •	_____ +	1.	• • •	_____ +
2.	_____		2.	K moves??	_____
	stalemate				

To Do Draw this otherwise losing position in one move, or win the White Queen in two moves.

Hint Use a Rook sacrifice check to force a Stalemate draw!

205

13 Zugzwang/Stalemate

Diagram 396

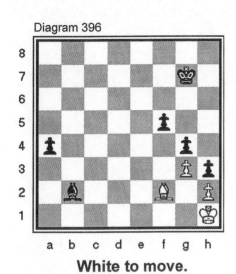

White to move.

	White	Black		White	Black
1.	_____ +	_____	1.	_____ +	Kf7??
		stalemate	2.	_____	

To Do Draw this otherwise losing position in one move, or win the Black Bishop in two moves.

Hint Use a Bishop sacrifice check to force a Stalemate draw.

Diagram 397

White to move.

	White	Black		White	Black
1.	_____ +	_____	1.	_____ +	Ka5/b6?
		stalemate	2.	_____	

To Do Draw this otherwise losing position in one move, or win the Black Bishop in two moves.

Hint Use a Bishop sacrifice check to force a Stalemate draw.

206

13 Zugzwang/Stalemate

Diagram 398

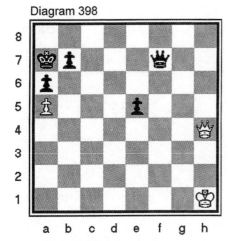

White to move.

	White		Black			White		Black
1.	_____	+	_____		1.	_____	+	Kb8??
			stalemate					
					2.	_____		

To Do Draw this otherwise losing position in one move, or win the Black Queen in two moves.

Hint Use a Queen sacrifice check to force a Stalemate draw.

Diagram 399

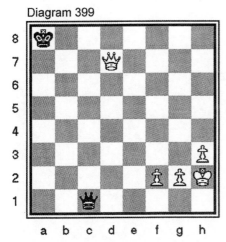

Black to move.

	White	Black			White	Black
1.	• • •	_____	+	1.	• • •	_____	+
2.	_____			2.	g3??	_____
	stalemate					

To Do Draw this otherwise losing position in one move, or win the White Queen in two moves.

Hint Use a Queen sacrifice check to force a Stalemate draw.

Diagram 400

a b c d e f g h

Black to move.

	White	Black		White	Black
1.	• • •	+	1.	• • •	+
2.	stalemate		2.	Ke7??	

To Do Draw this otherwise losing position in one move, or win the White Queen in two moves.

Hint Use a Queen sacrifice check to force a Stalemate draw.

Diagram 401

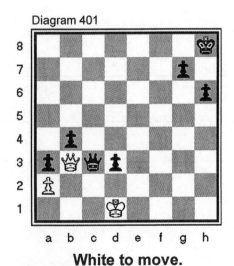

a b c d e f g h

White to move.

	White	Black
1.	+	stalemate

To Do Draw this otherwise losing position in one move.

Hint Use a Queen sacrifice check to force a Stalemate draw.

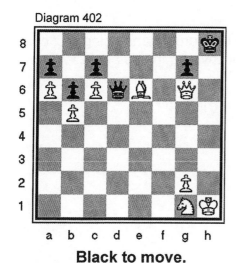

Diagram 402

Black to move.

	White	Black
1.	• • •	+
2.	_____	
	stalemate	

To Do Draw this otherwise losing position.

Hint Use a Queen sacrifice check to force a Stalemate draw.

Diagram 403

Black to move.

	White	Black		White	Black
1.	• • •	+	1.	• • •	+
2.	Kh2	+	2.	Kh2	+
3.	_____		3.	Kg3	+
	stalemate		4.	_____	
				stalemate	

To Do Draw this otherwise losing position in two or three moves.

Hint Begin with a pawn promotion and Queen check. Next, use one or two Queen sacrifice checks to force a Stalemate draw.

14 Quizzes: Identifying Tactics introduction

In this chapter are quizzes you can use to check your skill at naming and using tactics. Each problem can be solved by using one or more tactics covered in this book:

Pins
Back Rank Combinations
Knight Forks
Other Forks (Bishop Fork, etc.)
Discovered Checks
Double Checks
Discovered Attacks
Skewers
Double Threats
Promoting Pawns
Removing the Guard
Perpetual Check
Zugzwang/ Stalemate

Record the answer to each problem. Then, circle the tactic you used to solve it. Some problems may have more than one correct tactic.

Diagram 404

White to move.

To Do Win the Black Bishop in two moves.

	White	Black
1.	Bd6++	K moves
2.	Bxc5	

This one is done for you.

Circle the Tactic(s):

Pin
Back Rank Combination
Knight Fork
Other Fork
~~Discovered Check~~
~~Double Check~~
Discovered Attack

Skewer
Double Threat
Promoting a Pawn
Removing the Guard
Perpetual Check
Zugzwang/Stalemate

Record the answers to the problems and circle the tactic(s) used to solve them.

Diagram 405

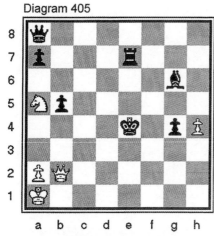

White to move.

To Do Win the Black Queen in two moves.

White	Black
1. _____ +	K moves
2. _____	

Circle the Tactic(s):

Pin   Skewer
Back Rank Combination   Double Threat
Knight Fork   Promoting a Pawn
Other Fork   Removing the Guard
Discovered Check   Perpetual Check
Double Check   Zugzwang/Stalemate
Discovered Attack

Diagram 406

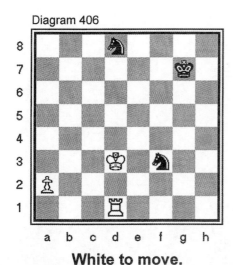

White to move.

To Do Win a Black Knight in two moves.

White	Black	White	Black
1. _____	Nf moves	1. _____	Nd moves
2. _____		2. _____	

Circle the Tactic(s):

Pin   Skewer
Back Rank Combination   Double Threat
Knight Fork   Promoting a Pawn
Other Fork   Removing the Guard
Discovered Check   Perpetual Check
Double Check   Zugzwang/Stalemate
Discovered Attack

14 Quizzes: Identifying Tactics

Record the answers to the problems and circle the tactic(s) used to solve them.

Diagram 407

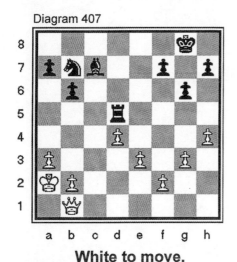

White to move.

To Do Win the Black Knight in two moves.

	White	Black
1.	________	R moves
2.	________	

Circle the Tactic(s):

Pin	Skewer
Back Rank Combination	Double Threat
Knight Fork	Promoting a Pawn
Other Fork	Removing the Guard
Discovered Check	Perpetual Check
Double Check	Zugzwang/Stalemate
Discovered Attack	

Diagram 408

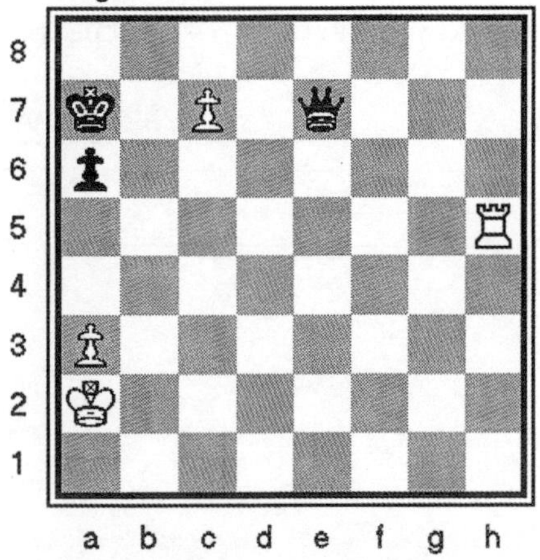

White to move.

To Do Win the Black Queen in two moves.

	White	Black
1.	________ +	K moves
2.	________	

Circle the Tactic(s):

Pin	Skewer
Back Rank Combination	Double Threat
Knight Fork	Promoting a Pawn
Other Fork	Removing the Guard
Discovered Check	Perpetual Check
Double Check	Zugzwang/Stalemate
Discovered Attack	

Record the answers to the problems and circle the tactic(s) used to solve them.

Diagram 409

White to move.

 Win the Black Queen for a Bishop in two moves.

	White	Black		White	Black
1.	_____ +	Qf6	1.	_____ +	Kg8??
2.	_____ +		2.	_____	

Circle the Tactic(s):

Pin	Skewer
Back Rank Combination	Double Threat
Knight Fork	Promoting a Pawn
Other Fork	Removing the Guard
Discovered Check	Perpetual Check
Double Check	Zugzwang/Stalemate
Discovered Attack	

Diagram 410

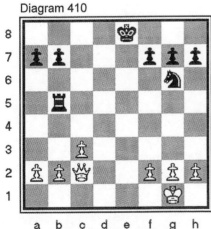

White to move.

 Win the Black Rook in three moves.

	White	Black
1.	_____	a6
2.	_____	Any move
3.	_____	

Circle the Tactic(s):

Pin	Skewer
Back Rank Combination	Double Threat
Knight Fork	Promoting a Pawn
Other Fork	Removing the Guard
Discovered Check	Perpetual Check
Double Check	Zugzwang/Stalemate
Discovered Attack	

14 Quizzes: Identifying Tactics

Record the answers to the problems and circle the tactic(s) used to solve them.

Diagram 411

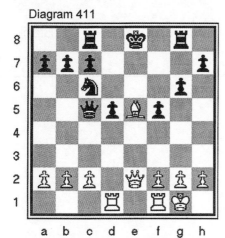

White to move.

	White	Black		White	Black
1.	______ +	K moves	1.	______ +	Ne7??
2.	______		2.	______ #	

To Do Win the Black Queen, or checkmate, in two moves.

Circle the Tactic(s):

Pin	Skewer
Back Rank Combination	Double Threat
Knight Fork	Promoting a Pawn
Other Fork	Removing the Guard
Discovered Check	Perpetual Check
Double Check	Zugzwang/Stalemate
Discovered Attack	

Diagram 412

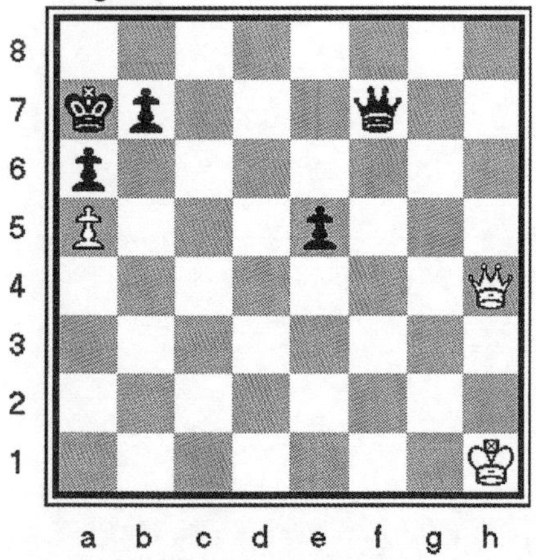

White to move.

	White	Black		White	Black
1.	______ +	______ stalemate	1.	______ +	Kb8??
			2.	______	

To Do Draw this otherwise losing position in one move, or win the Black Queen in two moves.

Circle the Tactic(s):

Pin	Skewer
Back Rank Combination	Double Threat
Knight Fork	Promoting a Pawn
Other Fork	Removing the Guard
Discovered Check	Perpetual Check
Double Check	Zugzwang/Stalemate
Discovered Attack	

Record the answers to the problems and circle the tactic(s) used to solve them.

Diagram 413

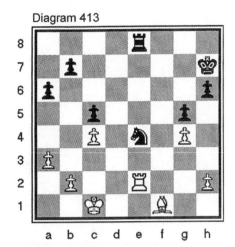

White to move.

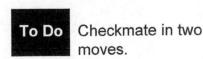 Win the Black Knight in three moves.

	White	Black
1.	_____	Rxe4
2.	_____	Any move
3.	_____	

Circle the Tactic(s):

Pin	Skewer
Back Rank Combination	Double Threat
Knight Fork	Promoting a Pawn
Other Fork	Removing the Guard
Discovered Check	Perpetual Check
Double Check	Zugzwang/Stalemate
Discovered Attack	

Diagram 414

White to move.

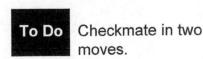 Checkmate in two moves.

	White	Black		White	Black
1.	++	Ke8	1.	++	Kc7
2.	#		2.	#	

Circle the Tactic(s):

Pin	Skewer
Back Rank Combination	Double Threat
Knight Fork	Promoting a Pawn
Other Fork	Removing the Guard
Discovered Check	Perpetual Check
Double Check	Zugzwang/Stalemate
Discovered Attack	

215

Record the answers to the problems and circle the tactic(s) used to solve them.

Diagram 415

White to move.

To Do Win the Black Queen and Black Knight for a Rook in three moves.

	White	Black
1.	_____ +	Nxh7
2.	_____ +	K moves
3.	_____	

Circle the Tactic(s):

Pin	Skewer
Back Rank Combination	Double Threat
Knight Fork	Promoting a Pawn
Other Fork	Removing the Guard
Discovered Check	Perpetual Check
Double Check	Zugzwang/Stalemate
Discovered Attack	

Diagram 416

Black to move.

To Do Win the White Queen for a Knight in two moves.

	White	Black		White	Black
1.	• • •	_____ +	1.	• • •	_____ +
2.	Bxg4	_____	2.	K moves?	_____

Circle the Tactic(s):

Pin	Skewer
Back Rank Combination	Double Threat
Knight Fork	Promoting a Pawn
Other Fork	Removing the Guard
Discovered Check	Perpetual Check
Double Check	Zugzwang/Stalemate
Discovered Attack	

Record the answers to the problems and circle the tactic(s) used to solve them.

Diagram 417

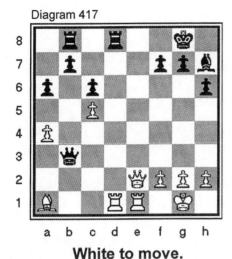

White to move.

 Checkmate in three moves.

	White	Black
1.	_____ +	_____
2.	_____ +	_____
3.	_____ #	

Circle the Tactic(s):

Pin	Skewer
Back Rank Combination	Double Threat
Knight Fork	Promoting a Pawn
Other Fork	Removing the Guard
Discovered Check	Perpetual Check
Double Check	Zugzwang/Stalemate
Discovered Attack	

Diagram 418

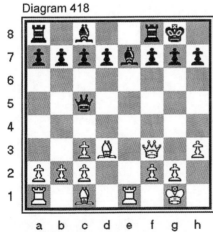

White to move.

 Win a Black Bishop in two moves or checkmate in three moves.

	White	Black		White	Black
1.	_____	Qh5	1.	_____	Re8??
2.	_____		2.	_____ +	Kf8
			3.	_____ #	

Circle the Tactic(s):

Pin	Skewer
Back Rank Combination	Double Threat
Knight Fork	Promoting a Pawn
Other Fork	Removing the Guard
Discovered Check	Perpetual Check
Double Check	Zugzwang/Stalemate
Discovered Attack	

Record the answers to the problems and circle the tactic(s) used to solve them.

Diagram 419

White to move.

 Win a pawn and the Black Bishop in two moves.

White		Black
1. _____	+	K moves
2. _____		

Circle the Tactic(s):

Pin	Skewer
Back Rank Combination	Double Threat
Knight Fork	Promoting a Pawn
Other Fork	Removing the Guard
Discovered Check	Perpetual Check
Double Check	Zugzwang/Stalemate
Discovered Attack	

Diagram 420

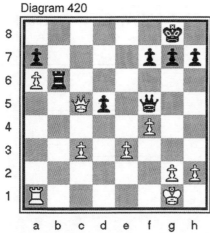

White to move.

 Promote the a-pawn in three moves.

White	Black
1. _____	axb6
2. _____	Any move
3. _____	

Circle the Tactic(s):

Pin	Skewer
~~Back Rank Combination~~	~~Double Threat~~
Knight Fork	Promoting a Pawn
Other Fork	Removing the Guard
Discovered Check	Perpetual Check
Double Check	Zugzwang/Stalemate
Discovered Attack	

Record the answers to the problems and circle the tactic(s) used to solve them.

Diagram 421

White to move.

To Do Win the Black Rook in three moves.

	White		Black
1.	_____	+	Kh7
2.	_____	+	g6
3.	_____		

Circle the Tactic(s):

Pin	Skewer
Back Rank Combination	Double Threat
Knight Fork	Promoting a Pawn
Other Fork	Removing the Guard
Discovered Check	Perpetual Check
Double Check	Zugzwang/Stalemate
Discovered Attack	

Diagram 422

White to move.

To Do Draw this otherwise losing position.

	White		Black
1.	_____	+	_____
2.	_____	+	_____
3.	_____	+	_____
4.	_____	+, etc.	
	draw		

Circle the Tactic(s):

Pin	Skewer
Back Rank Combination	Double Threat
Knight Fork	Promoting a Pawn
Other Fork	Removing the Guard
Discovered Check	Perpetual Check
Double Check	Zugzwang/Stalemate
Discovered Attack	

Record the answers to the problems and circle the tactic(s) used to solve them.

Diagram 423

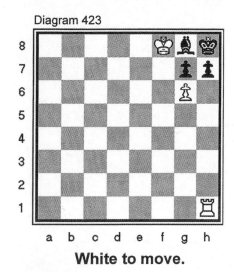

8 … ♔ ♝ ♚
7 … ♟ ♟
6 … ♙
5
4
3
2
1 … ♖

a b c d e f g h

White to move.

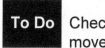 Checkmate in two moves.

	White	Black
1.	_____	g x h6
2.	_____ #	

	White	Black
1.	_____	B moves
2.	_____ #	

Circle the Tactic(s):

Pin	Skewer
Back Rank Combination	Double Threat
Knight Fork	Promoting a Pawn
Other Fork	Removing the Guard
Discovered Check	Perpetual Check
Double Check	Zugzwang/Stalemate
Discovered Attack	

Diagram 424

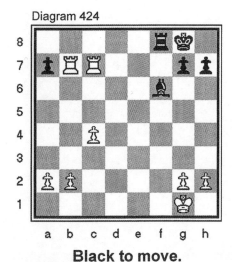

8 … ♜ ♚
7 ♟ ♖ ♖ … ♟ ♟
6 … ♝
5
4 … ♙
3
2 ♙ ♙ … ♙ ♙
1 … ♔

a b c d e f g h

Black to move.

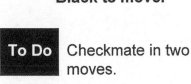 Checkmate in two moves.

	White	Black
1.	• • •	+
2.	_____	#

Circle the Tactic(s):

Pin	Skewer
Back Rank Combination	Double Threat
Knight Fork	Promoting a Pawn
Other Fork	Removing the Guard
Discovered Check	Perpetual Check
Double Check	Zugzwang/Stalemate
Discovered Attack	

14 Quizzes: Identifying Tactics

Record the answers to the problems and circle the tactic(s) used to solve them.

Diagram 425

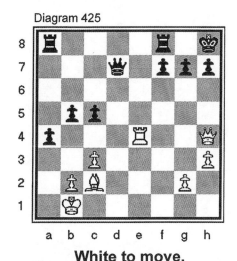

White to move.

To Do Win the Black Queen, or checkmate, in two moves.

	White	Black		White	Black
1.	_____	g6	1.	_____	Qxe7??
2.	_____		2.	___#___	

Circle the Tactic(s):

Pin	Skewer
Back Rank Combination	Double Threat
Knight Fork	Promoting a Pawn
Other Fork	Removing the Guard
Discovered Check	Perpetual Check
Double Check	Zugzwang/Stalemate
Discovered Attack	

Diagram 426

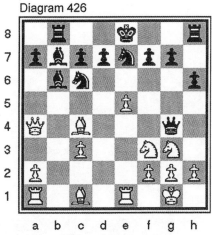

White to move.

To Do Win the Black Queen and a pawn for a Bishop in two moves.

	White	Black
1.	____+____	Kxf7
2.	_____	

Circle the Tactic(s):

Pin	Skewer
Back Rank Combination	Double Threat
Knight Fork	Promoting a Pawn
Other Fork	Removing the Guard
Discovered Check	Perpetual Check
Double Check	Zugzwang/Stalemate
Discovered Attack	

221

Record the answers to the problems and circle the tactic(s) used to solve them.

Diagram 427

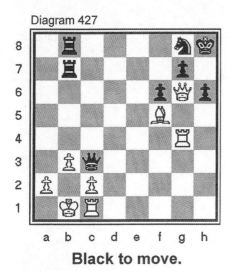

a b c d e f g h

Black to move.

 To Do Draw this otherwise losing position.

	White	Black
1.	• • •	_____ +
2.	a/cxb3	_____ +
3.	a/cxb3	_____ +
4.	Ka1	_____ +, etc.
		draw

Circle the Tactic(s):

Pin	Skewer
Back Rank Combination	Double Threat
Knight Fork	Promoting a Pawn
Other Fork	Removing the Guard
Discovered Check	Perpetual Check
Double Check	Zugzwang/Stalemate
Discovered Attack	

Diagram 428

a b c d e f g h

White to move.

 To Do Win the Black Knight in two moves.

	White	Black
1.	_____ +	Kxh7
2.	_____	

Circle the Tactic(s):

Pin	Skewer
Back Rank Combination	Double Threat
Knight Fork	Promoting a Pawn
Other Fork	Removing the Guard
Discovered Check	Perpetual Check
Double Check	Zugzwang/Stalemate
Discovered Attack	

14 Quizzes: Identifying Tactics

Record the answers to the problems and circle the tactic(s) used to solve them.

Diagram 429

White to move.

 Checkmate in three moves.

	White	Black
1.	_____ +	_____
2.	_____ +	_____
3.	_____ #	

Circle the Tactic(s):

Pin	Skewer
Back Rank Combination	Double Threat
Knight Fork	Promoting a Pawn
Other Fork	Removing the Guard
Discovered Check	Perpetual Check
Double Check	Zugzwang/Stalemate
Discovered Attack	

Diagram 430

Black to move.

To Do Win the White Bishop in three moves.

	White	Black
1.	• • • _____	_____
2.	_____	_____ +
3.	K moves _____	_____

Circle the Tactic(s):

Pin	Skewer
Back Rank Combination	Double Threat
Knight Fork	Promoting a Pawn
Other Fork	Removing the Guard
Discovered Check	Perpetual Check
Double Check	Zugzwang/Stalemate
Discovered Attack	

223

Record the answers to the problems and circle the tactic(s) used to solve them.

Diagram 431

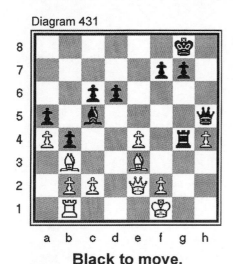

Black to move.

 To Do Win the White Queen for a Rook in two moves.

	White	Black
1.	• • •	_____ +
2.	_____	_____

Circle the Tactic(s):

Pin	Skewer
Back Rank Combination	Double Threat
Knight Fork	Promoting a Pawn
Other Fork	Removing the Guard
Discovered Check	Perpetual Check
Double Check	Zugzwang/Stalemate
Discovered Attack	

Diagram 432

White to move.

To Do Win the Black Bishop and pawn in three moves.

	White	Black
1.	_____	Rxh3
2.	_____ +	K moves
3.	_____	

Circle the Tactic(s):

Pin	Skewer
Back Rank Combination	Double Threat
Knight Fork	Promoting a Pawn
Other Fork	Removing the Guard
Discovered Check	Perpetual Check
Double Check	Zugzwang/Stalemate
Discovered Attack	

Record the answers to the problems and circle the tactic(s) used to solve them.

Diagram 433

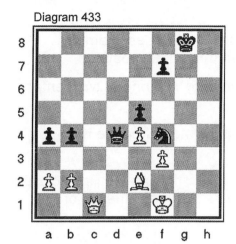

Black to move.

 Win the White Bishop in three moves.

	White	Black
1.	• • •	_____ +
2.	_____	_____ +
3.	K moves	_____

Circle the Tactic(s):

Pin	Skewer
Back Rank Combination	Double Threat
Knight Fork	Promoting a Pawn
Other Fork	Removing the Guard
Discovered Check	Perpetual Check
Double Check	Zugzwang/Stalemate
Discovered Attack	

Diagram 434

White to move.

 Win the Black Bishop in three moves.

	White	Black
1.	_____ +	Kxg7
2.	_____ +	K moves
3.	_____	

Circle the Tactic(s):

Pin	Skewer
Back Rank Combination	Double Threat
Knight Fork	Promoting a Pawn
Other Fork	Removing the Guard
Discovered Check	Perpetual Check
Double Check	Zugzwang/Stalemate
Discovered Attack	

Principles for Stronger Chess

Opening Principles

As a general rule, the opening consists of the first 10 or so moves of a chess game. The opening is the time when a player attempts to accomplish three main goals.

- Gain control of the important center squares (d4, e4, d5, and e5) with one or two center pawns (often called a *strong pawn center*).

- Develop Knights and Bishops to prepare for middle-game play and to free the King for castling.

- Castle early to protect the King and to develop the castled Rook, moving the Rook closer to open center files (c, d, e, and f). (An open file does not have a pawn of either color remaining on it.)

Middle-Game Principles

The middle game starts somewhere between the 10th and 20th move after center pawns have been moved, minor pieces (Knights and Bishops) have been developed, and pieces have been traded. The middle game has several goals:

- Place pawns to prevent the advance of enemy pieces onto your side of the board, and move your pieces in a way that gains space on your opponent's side of the board.

- Gain control of an open file with one or both Rooks. (Remember, an open file does not have a pawn of either color remaining on it.)

- Place Bishops on important open diagonals. (An open diagonal is one where no pawns are blocking the movement of the Bishop along the diagonal. Important open diagonals are those which run through one or more of the d4, e4, d5, and e5 center squares.)

- Create a Knight outpost if possible. (A Knight outpost is the placing of a Knight on a square where the opponent has no way of attacking it without losing a piece of greater value than the Knight. Usually the Knight is protected by a pawn.)

End-Game Principles

The end game starts when most of the pieces are off the board. Each player may only have two or three pawns left and perhaps one or two minor pieces. An important goal of the end-game is to use the King as a major attacking and defending piece.

- Move the King toward the center of the board where it can assist its own pawns in becoming Queens and prevent its opponent's pawns from reaching the eighth rank and becoming Queens.

Opening Principles Illustrated

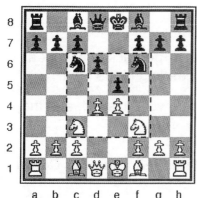

Each side has developed center pawns and two Knights.

Each side has castled after developing both Knights and Bishops.

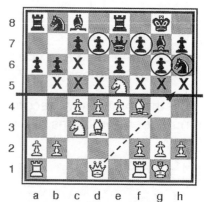

White has good center control, attacking 11 squares on Black's side of the board (X's and O's).

Middle-Game Principles Illustrated

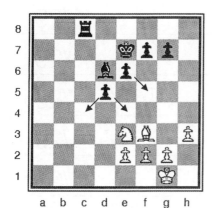

Black's pawns limit the movement of the White Bishop and Knight.

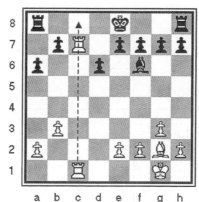

White's Rooks are doubled. They completely control the open c-file.

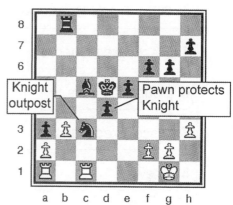

Black has a Knight outpost on c3, protected by the Black pawn on d4.

End-Game Principles Illustrated

The Black King is out of position to stop White's pawn advance.

The White King is in position both to advance the White e-pawn and to attack the Black pawns.

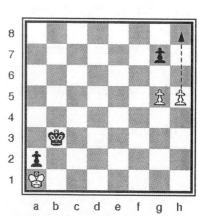

The Black King is not in position either to attack the White pawns or to help promote the pawn on a2.

227

Student Log
Chapter Problems

After completing and correcting the first five problems of each chapter, go back and work all of the problems, chapter by chapter. Correct each chapter before proceeding to the next.

On the form below, record the date you started each chapter, the date you finished, and the number of problems that you solved correctly.

Chapter	Diagrams	Date Started	Date Finished	Number Correct
1 Pins	3 to 31			/29
2 Back Rank Combin.	34 to 62			/29
3 Knight Forks	65 to 93			/29
4 Other Forks/D. Attacks	96 to 124			/29
5 Discovered Checks	127 to 155			/29
6 Double Checks	158 to 186			/29
7 Discovered Attacks	189 to 217			/29
8 Skewers	220 to 248			/29
9 Double Threats	251 to 279			/29
10 Promoting Pawns	282 to 310			/29
11 Removing the Guard	313 to 341			/29
12 Perpetual Check	344 to 372			/29
13 Zugzwang/Stalemate	375 to 403			/29
14 Quizzes	406 to 434			/29

Answer Key

Late 14th Century Chess Pieces. From left to right: Rook, Knight, and Bishop.

Students: To get the most out of your study of *Chess Tactics for Students*, work the first five problems in each chapter. Start with Chapter 1 and continue chapter-by-chapter through the book. After you complete the first five problems in each chapter, go back and finish each chapter. At each step, check your answers with the answers given in this Answer Key. Record your progress in the Student Log on page 228 of your book.

Page 2

Diagram 1

Circle the Black Queen.

Page 3

Diagram 2

1. Re1   Qxe1+ 1. Re1   0-0??
2. Qxe1+   2. Rxe4

Diagram 3

1. •••   Bd5   1. •••   Bd5
2. K m.   Bxe4 2. P m.   Bxe4+

Page 4

Diagram 4

1. Bb5   Qxb5 1. Bb5   Bd7
2. Nxb5   2. Bxc6

Page 4

Diagram 5

1. Rxe4   Rxe4
2. Bd3   Any move
3. Bxe4

Page 5

Diagram 6

1. •••   Bc7   1. •••   Bc7
2. K m.   Bxe5 2. P m.   Bxe5+

Diagram 7

1. Qa1   Any move
2. Qxd4

Page 6

Diagram 8

1. Rd4   K moves
2. Rxd5

Page 6

Diagram 9

1. d5   Bd7
2. dxc6

Page 7

Diagram 10

1. •••   Bb4
2. Bd2   Bxc3

Diagram 11

1. •••   Bc7   1. •••   Bc7
2. Kf4   Kf6   2. Kf4   Kf6
3. P m.   Bxe5+ 3. K m.   Bxe5

Page 8

Diagram 12

1. Ra8   Qxa8 1. Ra8   Qf8
2. Bxa8   2. Rxf8+

Page 8

Diagram 13

1. Re1   Qxe1+ 1. Re1   Ne7?
2. Qxe1+   2. Rxe5

Page 9

Diagram 14

1. Qa4   Ke7   1. Qa4   g4
2. Qxb5   2. Qxb5+ K m.
                3. hxg4

Diagram 15

1. •••   Qxf3+
2. Kxf3   Bb7
3. Any move Bxc6

Page 10

Diagram 16

1. Qa4   a6
2. c4   Any move
3. cxb5

Diagram 17

1. Nxd5   Qxd5??
2. Bc4   Qxc4
3. dxc4

Page 11

Diagram 18

1. Nxb4   cxb4   1. Nxb4   Any o.
2. Bxb6   2. Nd3!

Diagram 19

1. Nxe5   Qxe5? 1. Nxe5   0-0!
2. Re1   Qxe1+ 2. d4!
3. Qxe1+

Page 12

Diagram 20

1. d5   a6!
2. Bxc6+   Bxc6
3. dxc6

Page 12

Diagram 21

1. Qh4   Kg7
2. Rf1   Any move
3. Bxf6

Page 13

Diagram 22

1. Rd1   e5   1. Rd1   Qxc3?
2. Rxd4   2. Rxd7+ K m.
                 3. bxc3

Diagram 23

1. •••   Qg6
2. Kc2   c4
3. Any move cxd3

Page 14

Diagram 24

1. Bxe6   Qf6   1. Bxe6   dxe6??
2. Bxf7+   2. Rxd8+

Diagram 25

1. Nxf5   Nxf5?
2. Rf3   Any move
3. Rxf5

Page 15

Diagram 26

1. 0-0   Qxe4?? 1. 0-0   Qxe4??
2. Re1   Qxe1+   2. Re1   Nf6?
3. Qxe1+   3. Rxe4+

Diagram 27

1. •••   Qxc6
2. Qxc6   Bb7
3. Qxb7   Nxb7

Page 16

Diagram 28

1. Qh5+   Kg7/Kg8
2. Qxg6+   Kh8
3. Qh7#

Page 16

Diagram 29

1. Qxh7+   Kxh7
2. Rh5#

Page 17

Diagram 30

1. Rd8+   Kxd8
2. Qxc6

Diagram 31

1. c4   Nxc4   1. c4   Ne7
2. Rxd5   2. c5   Nbc8
                 3. cxd6

Page 18

Diagram 32

Circle the White Rook.

Page 19

Diagram 33

1. Qd8+   Rxd8
2. Rxd8#

Diagram 34

1. Rc8+   Bd8
2. Rxd8+   Re8
3. Rxe8#

Page 20

Diagram 35

1. Qf8+   Rxf8
2. Rxf8+   Qxf8
3. Rxf8#

Diagram 36

1. Qxe7   Rxe7??
2. Rd8+   Re8
3. Rxe8#

Page 21

Diagram 37

1. •••   Re1#

Page 21

Diagram 38

1. Qe8#

Page 22

Diagram 39

1. Qd8#

Diagram 40

1. Qxd8+   Rxd8
2. Rxd8#

Page 23

Diagram 41

1. Qe8+   Rxe8
2. Rxe8+   Rxe8
3. Rxe8#

Diagram 42

1. R/Qxf8+   Rxf8
2. R/Qxf8+   Qxf8
3. R/Qxf8#

The slash (/) is used to show that either
the Rook or Queen (R/Q) takes on f8.

Page 24

Diagram 43

1. Rxe8+   Qxe8
2. Rxe8#

Diagram 44

1. Rf8+   Rxf8
2. Rxf8#

Page 25

Diagram 45

1. R/Qb8+   Qxb8
2. R/Qxb8+   Re8
3. R/Qxe8#

Diagram 46

1. Ra8+   Qd8
2. Ra/dxd8+   Be8
3. Rxe8#

Page 26

Diagram 47

1. Rd8+   Rxd8
2. Rxd8#

Diagram 48

1. Rc8+   Nxc8
2. Rxc8+   Rd8
3. Rxd8#

Page 27

Diagram 49

1. •••   Rxa1+
2. Bc1   Rxc1+
3. Qd1   Rxd1#

Diagram 50

1. Re8+   Rxe8
2. dxe8=Q/R#

Page 28

Diagram 51

1. Rg8+   Rxg8
2. hxg8=Q/R#

Diagram 52

1. Qf8+   Bd8
2. Qxd8#

Page 29

Diagram 53

1. Rc8+   Be8
2. Rc/exe8#

Diagram 54

1. Qxa8+   Qc8
2. Qxc8+   Ne8
3. Q/Rxe8#

Page 30

Diagram 55

1. •••   Bd4+
2. Kh1   Rf1#

Page 30

Diagram 56

1. Re8+   Nxe8
2. Rxe8+   Bf8
3. Rxf8#

Page 31

Diagram 57

1. •••   Qxg1+
2. Kxg1   Rc1#

Diagram 58

1. Qxf8+   Rxf8
2. Rxf8#

Page 32

Diagram 59

1.	•••	Bxd4+	1.	•••	Bxd4+
2.	Kh1	Rf1+	2.	Re3	Bxe3+
3.	Rxf1	Rxf1#	3.	Kh1	Rf1#

Diagram 60

1.	•••	Qd4+	1.	•••	Qd4+
2.	Bxd4	Bxd4+	2.	Bxd4	Bxd4+
3.	kh1	Rf1+	3.	Re3	Bxe3+
4.	Rxf1	Rxf1#	4.	Kh1	Rf1#

Page 33

Diagram 61

1. Qxd8+   Nxd8
2. Re8#

Diagram 62

1. Rxd8+   Rxd8
2. Qe8+   Rxe8
3. Rxe8#

Page 34

Diagram 63

Circle the White Knight.

Page 35

Diagram 64

1. Nd6+   K moves
2. Nxb7

Diagram 65

1. Ngf6+   gxf6
2. Ndxf6+   K moves
3. Nxd7

Page 36

Diagram 66

1. Bxf7+   Kxf7
2. Nxe5+   K moves
3. Nxc6

Diagram 67

1. Qxd4+   Qxd4
2. Nf5+   K moves
3. Nxd4

Page 37

Diagram 68

1. •••   Ne3+
2. K moves   Nxg2

Diagram 69

1. Nc6   Kf6
2. Nxa7

Page 38

Diagram 70

1. Nc7+   K moves
2. Nxd5

Diagram 71

1. Nc7+   K moves
2. Nxa8

Page 39

Diagram 72

1. Nc7+   K moves
2. Nxe6

Page 39

Diagram 73

1. Nf5+   K moves
2. Nxe7

Page 40

Diagram 74

1. Nd5+   K moves
2. Nxc7

Diagram 75

1. •••   Nf2+
2. K moves   Nxd1

Page 41

Diagram 76

1. Nd6+ K m.   1. Nd6+ Bxd6??
2. Nxb7   2. Bxd8

Diagram 77

1. •••   Nec3+
2. bxc3   Nxc3+
3. K moves   Nxe2

Page 42

Diagram 78

1. •••   Bxc2+
2. Kxc2   Nxd4+
3. K moves   Nxf3

Diagram 79

1. Rxc6+   Qxc6
2. Ne7+   K moves
3. Nxc6

Page 43

Diagram 80

1. Rxf8+   Rxf8
2. Rxf8+   Qxf8
3. Nxg6+   K moves
4. Nxf8

Page 43

Diagram 81

1. Nbd6+   Bxd6?
2. Nxd6+   K moves
3. Nxf7   Rhe8
4. Nxd8

Page 44

Diagram 82

1. Qxb7   Bxb7
2. Nf7+   K moves
3. Nxd8

Diagram 83

1. Qxg7+   Kxg7
2. Ne6+   K moves
3. Nxd8

Page 45

Diagram 84

1. Qxd5   Qxd5
2. Nf6+   K moves
3. Nxd5

Diagram 85

1. •••   Qxe4
2. Nxe4   Ne2+
3. K moves   Nxc3

Page 46

Diagram 86

1. Qxc6   Qxc6?
2. Nxe7+   Kh8
3. Nxc6

Diagram 87

1. •••   Qg1+
2. Kxg1   Nxe2+
3. K moves   Nxc1

Page 47

Diagram 88
1. Qxc8+   Rxc8
2. Ne6+   K moves
3. N/Rxg7

Diagram 89
1. •••   Qxf3
2. gxf3   Ne2+
3. K moves   Nxd4

Page 48

Diagram 90
1. Qxc8   Rxc8
2. Nd7+   K moves
3. Nxb6

Diagram 91
1. •••   Qxg3+
2. Kxg3   Ne4+
3. K moves   Nxd2

Page 49

Diagram 92
1. Rxd5   Bxd5
2. Nf4+   K moves
3. Nxd5

Diagram 93
1. ••• Nc5   1. ••• Nc5
2. Rbb1 Nd3   2. Rbb1 Nd3
3. Be3 Nxc1 3. Rcc2 Nxf4

Page 50

Diagram 94
Circle the White Rook and Bishop.

Page 51

Diagram 95
1. ••• Ke5   1. ••• Ke5
2. B m. Kxf4 2. g3   Kxd5

Page 51

Diagram 96
1. d4   N m.   1. d4   Bxd4
2. dxe5   2. exd4

Page 52

Diagram 97
1. Rb7+   K moves
2. Rxa7

Diagram 98
1. c5   Bxc5   1. c5   Bxc5
2. d4   Bxd4   2. d4   N m.
3. exd4   3. dxc5

Page 53

Diagram 99
1. Qe2+   K moves
2. Qxh5

Diagram 100
1. Qd8+   Kh7
2. Qxa5

Page 54

Diagram 101
1. Qd8+   K moves/Nf8
2. Qxg5

Diagram 102
1. Qc2+ K m./g6 1. Qc2+ Be4
2. Qxc6   2. Qxe4+

Page 55

Diagram 103
1. Bxg6+   Kxg6
2. Qc2+   K moves
3. Qxc5

Page 55

Diagram 104
1. Rxg7+   Kxg7
2. Qd4+   K moves
3. Qxa7

Page 56

Diagram 105
1. Qxe6+ Kf8 1. Qxe6+ Kd8
2. Qxc8+ Kg7 2. Qxg8+ Kc7
3. Qb7+ Kh6 3. Qxa2
4. Qxb6

Diagram 106
1. •••   Re2+ 1. •••   Rb7
2. K m. Rxb2 2. N m. Rxb2+

Page 57

Diagram 107
1. Rd7 Kg8   1. Rd7 b6/Rb8
2. Rxb7   2. Rxh7

Diagram 108
1. Rg5+   K moves
2. Rxg4

Page 58

Diagram 109
1. Nxg4   Nxg4
2. Rg5+   K moves
3. Rxg4

Diagram 110
1. Nxb7 Bxb7 1. Nxb7 a5?
2. Rc7+ K m. 2. Nxa5! Bxa5
3. Rxb7   3. Rc5! Be6
              4. Rxa5

Page 59

Diagram 111
1. Bxd5   exd5
2. Re7+   K moves
3. Rxb7

Page 59

Diagram 112

1.	Be5	N m.	1.	Be5	P m.
2.	Bxc7		2.	Bxg3	

Page 60

Diagram 113

1. Bxc6+   K moves
2. Bxe4

Diagram 114

1. Rxh3   Rxh3
2. Bxe6+   K moves
3. Bxh3

Page 61

Diagram 115

1. Ra8+   Kh7
2. Be4+   g6/f5
3. Bxd3

Diagram 116

1. Nxd3   Rxd3?
2. Ra8+   Kh7
3. Be4+   g6/f5
4. Bxd3

Page 62

Diagram 117

1. •••   Rxg3
2. Rxg3?   Bxf4+
3. K moves   Bxg3

Diagram 118

1.	Bxe5+	K m.	1.	Bxe5+	Nxe5??
2.	Bxb8		2.	Rc7+	Qxc7
			3.	Qxc7	

Page 63

Diagram 119

1.	e5	Be7	1.	e5	Bxe5
2.	exf6		2.	dxe5	

Page 63

Diagram 120

1. •••   c5
2. Nf3   c4
3. Q moves   cxb3

Page 64

Diagram 121

1.	f4	Bd6	1.	f4	Bd6
2.	e5	N m.	2.	e5	Be7
3.	exd6		3.	exf6	

Diagram 122

1. •••   Bxf4+
2. Kxf4   g5+
3. K moves   gxh4

Page 65

Diagram 123

1.	Kb2	N m.	1.	Kb2	B m.
2.	Kxb1		2.	Kxc1	

Diagram 124

1.	Kb3	Rc3+?	1.	Kb3	N m.?
2.	Kxa2		2.	Kxc4	

Page 66

Diagram 125

Circle the White Rook.

Page 67

Diagram 126

1.	Bd3+	K m.	1.	Bg8+	Qc2
2.	Bxh7		2.	Rxc2+	

Diagram 127

1.	Bb5+	Kf8	1.	Bb5+	Be6
2.	Bxc6		2.	Bxc6+	

Page 68

Diagram 128

1. Nxe5+   Kh8
2. Nxg4

Diagram 129

1.	Rh8+	Kxh8	1.	Rh8+	Kxh8
2.	Bxg7+	Rxg7	2.	Bxg7+	Kxg7
3.	Qxd5		3.	Qxd5	

Page 69

Diagram 130

1. Bf6#

Diagram 131

1. Bf8#

Page 70

Diagram 132

1. •••   Bg6#

Diagram 133

1. •••   e2+
2. Kh1   e1=Q/R#

Page 71

Diagram 134

1.	d5+	Qf6	1.	d5+	Kg8??
2.	Bxf6		2.	dxe6	

Diagram 135

1.	Qxd7+	Kxd7	1.	Qxd7+	Kxd7
2.	dxc5+	Kc6	2.	dxc5+	Qd6?
3.	dxb6		3.	R/cxd6	

Page 72

Diagram 136

1.	d7+	Ka8	1.	d7+	Rc7??
2.	dxc8=Q/R+		2.	Qxh8+	

Page 72

Diagram 137

1. Qxf8   Qxf8
2. c8=Q/R+   Kg8
3. Q/Rxf8+

Page 73

Diagram 138

1. Ne5+   K moves
2. Nxf7

Diagram 139

1. Nc6+   Be7   1. Nc6+   Qe7
2. Nxd8   2. Nxe7

Page 74

Diagram 140

1. Nc5+   Qe6   1. Nc5+   Be6
2. Nxe6   2. Nxa6

Diagram 141

1. Ne4+ K m./ f6   1. Ne4+ Qd4/c3/b2?
2. Nxd2   2. Bxd4/c3/b2+

Page 75

Diagram 142

1. Qxb7+ Kxb7   1. Qxb7+ Kxb7
2. Nc4+   K m.   2. Nc4+   Qb3/b4'
3. Nxa3   3. Rxb3/b4+

Diagram 143

1. Rxh6+   Kxh6
2. Nxd5+   Any move
3. Nxe7

Page 76

Diagram 144

1. Na5+   Kb8   1. Na5+   Kd8
2. Qb5#   2. Nxc6#

Page 76

Diagram 145

1. Nh6++ Kh8   1. Nh6++ Kf8?
2. Qg8+   R/Nxg8 2. Qf7#
3. Nf7#

Page 77

Diagram 146

1. Bd6+   K m.   1. Bd6+   Ne7??
2. Bxc5   2. Qxe7#

Diagram 147

1. •••   Bxc2+   1. •••   Bxc2+
2. Qf3   Rxf3+   2. K m.? Bxb3

Page 78

Diagram 148

1. Be8/d5+ K m. 1. Be8/d5+ Ne7
2. Bxc6   2. Rxe7+

Diagram 149

1. b4   Nc6   1. b4   Nb3/c4
2. Be8/d5+   K m.   2. Bxb3/c4+
3. Bxc6

Page 79

Diagram 150

1. Rxb6+   K moves
2. Rxb7

Diagram 151

1. Rf1+   K moves
2. Rxc1

Page 80

Diagram 152

1. Qxb6   cxb6
2. Re1+   K moves
3. Rxf1

Page 80

Diagram 153

1. Rxg7+   Kh8
2. Rg8++   Kxg8
3. Rg1#

Page 81

Diagram 154

1. Rxb7+   Kg8
2. Rg7+   Kh8
3. Rxa7+   Kg8
4. Rxa8+

Diagram 155

1. Rxf7+   Kg8
2. Rg7+   Kh8
3. Rxg6+   Rf6
4. Bxf6#

Page 82

Diagram 156

Circle the White Queen and the White Knight.

Page 83

Diagram 157

1. Nf6#

Diagram 158

1. Bb5#

Page 84

Diagram 159

1. Bg5++ Ke8   1. Bg5++ Kc7
2. Rd8#   2. Bd8#

Diagram 160

1. Qd8+   Kxd8   1. Qd8+   Kxd8
2. Bg5++ Ke8   2. Bg5++ Kc7
3. Rd8#   3. Bd8#

Page 85

Diagram 161

1. ...   Nf3#

Diagram 162

1. Nf6#

Page 86

Diagram 163

1. Ng6#

Diagram 164

1. ...   Rxf1#

Page 87

Diagram 165

1. Nc5++   Kb8
2. Na6#

Diagram 166

1. Rb8+   Kxb8   1. Rb8+   Rxb8
2. Nxd7++   2. Nxd7

Page 88

Diagram 167

1. Qg7+   Kxg7
2. Nf5++   Kg8
3. Nh6#

Diagram 168

1. Bxf7+   Kxf7   1. Bxf7+   Kxf7
2. Ne5++ Ke8/Kf6   2. Nd6++ Kf6/Kg6
3. Qf7#   3. Qf7#

Page 89

Diagram 169

1. Nxf7+   Kg8   1. Nxf7+   Kg8
2. Nh6++   Kh8   2. Nh6++   Kf8?
3. Qg8+!   Rxg8   3. Qf7#
4. Nf7#

Page 89

Diagram 170

1. Qxh7+   Kxh7
2. Nf6++   Kh8
3. Ng6#

Page 90

Diagram 171

1. Bd6++   K moves
2. Bxc5

Diagram 172

1. ...   Bd3++
2. Ke1   Rf1#

Page 91

Diagram 173

1. Bg5++   Ke8
2. Rd8#

Diagram 174

1. Qd8+   Kxd8
2. Bg5++   Ke8
3. Rd8#

Page 92

Diagram 175

1. ...   Bd4++
2. Kd1   Re1#

Diagram 176

1. ... Qxd4   1. ...   Qxd4
2. Bd3! Qg4/d6/b6 2. exd4?? Bb4++
                      3. Kd1   Re1#

Page 93

Diagram 177

1. Ba5++   Kc8/Ke8
2. Rd8#

Page 93

Diagram 178

1. Qd8+   Kxd8
2. Ba5++   Kc8/Ke8
3. Rd8#

Page 94

Diagram 179

1. Bg5++   Ke8
2. Rd8#

Diagram 180

1. Qd8+   Kxd8
2. Bg5++   Ke8
3. Rd8#

Page 95

Diagram 181

1. Nf5+   exf5
2. Bc5#

Diagram 182

1. Nf6+   Bxf6?   1. Nf6+   Qxf6
2. Bb5#   2. Qd8+! Bxd8
                      3. Bb5#

Page 96

Diagram 183

1. Bxf7++ Kd8   1. Bxf7++ Kxf7??
2. Qe8+   Kc7   2. Qe6#
3. Qxa8

Diagram 184

1. ...   Qg2+
2. Kxg2   Rxg3#

Page 97

Diagram 185

1. Rg8++   Kxg8
2. Rg1#

Page 97

Diagram 186

1. Rg8++ Kxg8
2. Rg1#

Page 98

Diagram 187

Circle the White Queen.

Page 99

Diagram 188

1. Bb5+ Ke7	1. Bb5+ Bd7
2. Qxd4	2. Bxd7+ Kxd7
	3. Qxd4

Diagram 189

1. Ba6 Q moves
2. Bxc8

Page 100

Diagram 190

1. Bxa7+ Kxa7/Ka8
2. Qxh3

Diagram 191

1. Nxe5 Qxe5??
2. Nb5+ axb5
3. Bxe5

Page 101

Diagram 192

1. c4 Q moves
2. cxd5

Diagram 193

1. d5 Q m.	1. d5 Nxd5
2. Bxb6	2. Nxd5/Qxd5

Page 102

Diagram 194

1. ••• Ng4+	1. ••• Ng4+
2. Bxg4+ Bxd4	2. K m. Bxd4

Page 102

Diagram 195

1. ••• Rxd4
2. Qxd4?? Ng4+
3. Bxg4 Bxd4

Page 103

Diagram 196

1. Nh6+ gxh6
2. Qxd7

Diagram 197

1. ••• Nh3+
2. K moves Qxd2

Page 104

Diagram 198

1. ••• Bxh2+
2. Kxh2 Rxe4

Diagram 199

1. Bxg7 Kxg7
2. Rxc6

Page 105

Diagram 200

1. Bc7 R moves
2. Rxd7

Diagram 201

1. Bf4 Q m.	1. Bf4 Bd6?
2. Bxb8	2. R/Bxd6

Page 106

Diagram 202

1. Bxh7+ Kxh7
2. Rxd8

Diagram 203

1. Bc4+ K m.	1. Bc4+ Be6?
2. Rxa7	2. Bxe6+ Qxe6
	3. Rxa7

Page 107

Diagram 204

1. Bb4 Rxe4
2. Bxa5

Diagram 205

1. Be7 Re8?
2. Bb4 Rxe4
3. Bxa5

Page 108

Diagram 206

1. Bh7+ K/Nxh7
2. Qxd4

Diagram 207

1. Bxf7+ Kxf7
2. Qxd6

Page 109

Diagram 208

1. Bxe6+ Bxe6
2. Qxc7

Diagram 209

1. Nxc7 Qxc7??
2. Bxe6+ Bxe6
3. Qxc7

Page 110

Diagram 210

1. Be6+ K moves
2. Qxc5

Diagram 211

1. Rxc8+ Kxc8
2. Be6+ K moves
3. Qxc5

Page 111

Diagram 212

1. ••• Bxh2+
2. Kxh2 Qxa6

Page 111

Diagram 213

1. •••	Ba6	1. •••	Ba6
2. Qxa6?	Bxh2+	2. Qc2	Bxf1
3. Kxh2	Qxa6		

Page 112

Diagram 214

1. Bxf7+   Kxf7
2. Qxg4

Diagram 215

1. •••   d5
2. Q moves   Bxa3

Page 113

Diagram 216

1. Re8+   Rxe8
2. Qxd5

Diagram 217

1. Ke3	Nf m.	1. Ke3	Nd m.
2. Rxd8		2. Kxf3	

Page 114

Diagram 218

Circle the White Rook.

Page 115

Diagram 219

1. Re1+   K moves
2. Rxe8

Diagram 220

1. Bc4+   K moves
2. Bxg8

Page 116

Diagram 221

1. Qe4   R moves
2. Qxb7

Page 116

Diagram 222

1. •••	Qxf1+	1. •••	Qxf1+
2. Kxf1	Rd1+	2. Kxf1	Rd1+
3. Ke2	Re1+	3. Re1??	Rxe1#
4. K m.	Rxe6		

Page 117

Diagram 223

1. Bg2+   K moves
2. Bxa8

Diagram 224

1. Bb3+   K moves
2. Bxf7

Page 118

Diagram 225

1. •••   Bg5+
2. K moves   Bxc1

Diagram 226

1. •••   Rxd2
2. Kxd2   Bg5+
3. K moves   Bxc1

Page 119

Diagram 227

1. •••   Bf5+
2. K moves   Bxb1

Diagram 228

1. •••   Rxf3+
2. Kxf3   Bg4+
3. K moves   Bxd1

Page 120

Diagram 229

1. Bd6   Q moves
2. Bxb8

Page 120

Diagram 230

1. dxe5   dxe5
2. Bd6   Q moves
3. Bxb8

Page 121

Diagram 231

1. •••   Be6
2. Qe2   Bxa2

Diagram 232

1. •••   Nxc4
2. Qxc4   Be6
3. Qe2   Bxa2

Page 122

Diagram 233

1. •••   Bg4
2. Q moves   Bxd1

Diagram 234

1. Bd5   R moves
2. Bxb7

Page 123

Diagram 235

1. Bb4	Rdd8	1. Bb4	Rfd8
2. Bxf8		2. Bxd6	

Diagram 236

1. Be8	Rgh6	1. Be8	Rhg5
2. Bxh5		2. Bxg6	

Page 124

Diagram 237

1. Ba5	Rcd7	1. Ba5	Rdc8
2. Bxd8		2. Bxc7	

Diagram 238

1. Qxa6	bxa6	1. Qxa6	bxa6
2. Ba5	Rcd7	2. Ba5	Rdc8
3. Bxd8		3. Bxc7	

Page 125

Diagram 239
1. Rh7+   K moves
2. Rxb7

Diagram 240
1. Rh7+   Nxh7
2. Rxh7+   K moves
3. Rxb7

Page 126

Diagram 241
1. Re5   Q moves
2. Rxa5

Diagram 242
1. Rh5   Q moves
2. Rxa5

Page 127

Diagram 243
1. Rxe5   dxe5
2. Rd1+   K moves
3. Rxd8

Diagram 244
1. •••   Nc6+
2. Bxc6   Rb1+
3. K moves   Rxb8

Page 128

Diagram 245
1. Qg8+   Kd6
2. Qxb3

Diagram 246
1. Ne5+   Ke6
2. Qg8+   K moves
3. Qxb3

Page 129

Diagram 247
1. Qg2+   K moves
2. Qxa8

Diagram 248
1. Qh3+   K moves
2. Qxc8

Page 130

Diagram 249
Circle the c8 square.

Page 131

Diagram 250
1. Rc5   Ba1??   1. Rc5   K m.
2. Rc8#   2. Rxc3

Diagram 251
1. Be4   R m.??   1. Be4   N m.
2. Rh7#   2. Bxb1

Page 132

Diagram 252
1. Qd4   Nb5??   1. Qd4   f6
2. Qg7/h8#   2. Qxa7

Diagram 253
1. Re7   Qxe7??   1. Re7   g6/h6
2. Qxh7#   2. Rxd7

Page 133

Diagram 254
1. •••   Rb4   1. •••   Rb4
2. Ba8??   Rb1#   2. K m.   Rxb7

Diagram 255
1. Bc7   Qxc7??   1. Bc7   h6
2. Rf8#   2. Bxb6

Page 134

Diagram 256
1. •••   Rf2   1. •••   Rf2
2. Qxe1??   Rh2#   2. Qxf2   Qxf2

Diagram 257
1. Qe5   Qxe5??   1. Qe5   Rxf7
2. Rxf8#   2. Qxc5

Page 135

Diagram 258
1. Bg8   Qxd4??   1. Bg8   Kxg8
2. Qxh7#   2. Rxd6

Diagram 259
1. Nf5   Nxf5??   1. Nf5   f6
2. Qh8#   2. Nxe7

Page 136

Diagram 260
1. •••   Be5   1. •••   Be5
2. Rd7??   Rxh2#   2. N m.   Bxc7

Diagram 261
1. •••   Qe7   1. •••   Qe7
2. Rxd4??   Qe1#   2. Nf2   Qxh4

Page 137

Diagram 262
1. Qf5   R m.??   1. Qf5   g6
2. Qxh7#   2. Qxc8+

Diagram 263
1. Qg5   g6??   1. Qg5   Kf8
2. Qxd8+   Qe8   2. Qxd8+
3. Qxe8#

Page 138

Diagram 264
1. •••   Qe7   1. •••   Qe7
2. Ra6??   Qe2#   2. Bf5   Qxa3

Page 138

Diagram 265

1.	•••	Qc7+	1.	•••	Qc7+
2.	g3	Qe7	2.	g3	Qe7
3.	Ra6??	Qe2#	3.	Bf5	Qxa3

Page 139

Diagram 266

| 1. | Nf6 | Nxf5?? | 1. | Nf6 | Bg7 |
| 2. | Rh7# | | 2. | Bxb1 | |

Diagram 267

| 1. | Qe4 | Rc3?? | 1. | Qe4 | Bf5 |
| 2. | Qxh7# | | 2. | Qxc6 | |

Page 140

Diagram 268

| 1. | Qe5 | Red8?? | 1. | Qe5 | f6 |
| 2. | Qxg7# | | 2. | Qxd6 | |

Diagram 269

1.	Rxd6	Rxd6?	1.	Rxd6	Rxd6?
2.	Qe5	Red8??	2.	Qe5	f6
3.	Qxg7#		3.	Qxd6	

Page 141

Diagram 270

| 1. | ••• | Qe5 | 1. | ••• | Qe5 |
| 2. | Rd3?? | Qh2# | 2. | g3/f4 | Qxd4 |

Diagram 271

1.	•••	Rxd4	1.	•••	Rxd4
2.	Rxd4?	Qe5	2.	Rxd4?	Qe5
3.	Rd3??	Qh2#	3.	g3/f4	Qxd4

Page 142

Diagram 272

| 1. | Qe4 | c5?? | 1. | Qe4 | f5/g6 |
| 2. | Qxh7# | | 2. | Qxd4 | |

Page 142

Diagram 273

1.	Qe4	Re8??	1.	Qe4	Qh5
2.	Qxh7+	Kf8	2.	Qxe7	
3.	Qh8#				

Page 143

Diagram 274

| 1. | ••• | Rd3 | 1. | ••• | Rd3 |
| 2. | Rac1?? | Rh3# | 2. | Kh2 | Rxc3 |

Diagram 275

| 1. | Qd4 | Nxf1?? | 1. | Qd4 | f6 |
| 2. | Qxg7# | | 2. | Qxe3 | |

Page 144

Diagram 276

| 1. | ••• | Qc4 | 1. | ••• | Qc4 |
| 2. | Nf3?? | Qxf1+ | 2. | Qf3 | Q/Bxh4 |

Diagram 277

| 1. | ••• | Qe3 | 1. | ••• | Qe3 |
| 2. | Rxe3?? | Rf1# | 2. | Qd1 | Qxg5 |

Page 145

Diagram 278

| 1. | ••• | Be4 | 1. | ••• | Be4 |
| 2. | Qxa7?? | Nh3# | 2. | Qxe4 | Nxe4 |

Diagram 279

1.	Ne5	Nxe5??	1.	Ne5	Kg8
2.	Qxh5+	Kg8	2.	Nxd7	
3.	Qh8#				

Page 146

Diagram 280

Circle the White Pawn on a6.

Page 147

Diagram 281

1.	Bxb6	axb6
2.	a7	K/B moves
3.	a8=Q	

Diagram 282

1.	Nxf6	gxf6
2.	g7	K/N moves
3.	g8=Q	

Page 148

Diagram 283

1.	Qxb6	axb6
2.	a7	Any move
3.	a8=Q	

Diagram 284

| 1. | f8=R | Kh6 | 1. | f8=Q?? | |
| 2. | Rh8# | | | | stalemate |

Page 149

Diagram 285

| 1. | c8=N+ | K moves |
| 2. | Nxe7 | |

Diagram 286

| 1. | d8=N+ | K moves |
| 2. | Nxf7 | |

Page 150

Diagram 287

1.	•••	Bxg3
2.	hxg3	h2
3.	Any move	h1=Q

Diagram 288

1.	•••	Ba4
2.	bxa4	b3
3.	axb3	a2
4.	Any move	a1=Q

Page 151

Diagram 289

1.	Bd4	Bxd4	1.	Bd4	Kb6?
2.	f8=Q		2.	Bxc5+	Kxc5
			3.	f8=Q+	

Diagram 290

1.	Bf4	Kxf4
2.	h6	Any move
3.	h7	Any move
4.	h8=Q	

Page 152

Diagram 291

1.	Nxg7	Nxg7
2.	h6	N moves
3.	h7	Any move
4.	h8=Q	

Diagram 292

1.	•••	Re1	1.	•••	Re1
2.	Rxe1	Nxe1	2.	Ne2?	Rxg1
3.	Kxe1	h2	3.	Nxg1	h2
4.	Any m.	h1=Q	4.	Any m.	h1=Q

Page 153

Diagram 293

1.	Rd8+	Rxd8	1.	Rd8+	Rxd8
2.	Rf8+	Kxf8	2.	Rf8+	Kd7??
3.	cxd8=Q+		3.	cxd8=Q+	

Diagram 294

1.	Rd6+	Rxd6
2.	b8=Q	

Page 154

Diagram 295

1.	•••	Qxd1
2.	Qxd1	a1=Q

Page 154

Diagram 296

1.	•••	Qxf1+
2.	Qxf1	Re1+
3.	Qxe1	fxe1=Q+

Page 155

Diagram 297

1.	Qxd5	cxd5
2.	a6	Any move
3.	a7	Any move
4.	a8=Q	

Diagram 298

1.	Qxd6+	Qxd6	1.	Qxd6+	Qxd6
2.	c7	Any m.	2.	c7	Qxc7?
3.	c8=Q		3.	Rxc7	

Page 156

Diagram 299

1.	Qxe6	fxe6
2.	f7	Qg7
3.	f8=Q	

Diagram 300

1.	Qc8+	Kh7
2.	Qxe6	fxe6
3.	f7	Qg7
4.	f8=Q	

Page 157

Diagram 301

1.	Qe5+	Kg8
2.	Qe8+	Qxe8
3.	dxe8=Q+	

Diagram 302

1.	Qe6+	Qxe6
2.	dxe6	Any move
3.	e8=Q	

Page 158

Diagram 303

1.	Bg7	Kd7	1.	Bg7	Nxg7??
2.	f8=Q	Nxf8	2.	f8=Q+	
3.	Bxf8				

Diagram 304

1.	Bc4+	Kh8	1.	Bc4+	Nxc4??
2.	Bb5/f7	g6	2.	e8=Q#	
3.	e8=Q	Nxe8			
4.	Bxe8				

Page 159

Diagram 305

1.	e7	Qd7	1.	e7	Re8?
2.	exd8=Q+		2.	Qxd3	

Diagram 306

1.	•••	e4+
2.	Bxe4	Nxe4
3.	Any move	c2
4.	Any move	c1=Q

Page 160

Diagram 307

1.	•••	f1=N#

Diagram 308

1.	e8=N	Any move
2.	Nc7#	

Page 161

Diagram 309

1.	c8=R		1.	c8=Q??
				stalemate

Diagram 310

1.	f8=N+	Kh8
2.	Bd4+	Qe5
3.	Bxe5#	

Page 162

Diagram 311

Circle the White Queen.

Page 163

Diagram 312

1. Rc8+   Rxc8
2. Qxb2

Diagram 313

1. Qg4+   Qxg4
2. Rxe8+   Kg7
3. fxg4

Page 164

Diagram 314

1. •••   Rg1+
2. Kxg1   Qxe2

Diagram 315

1. Re7   Qxe7
2. Qxd5+   Any move
3. Qxa8+

Page 165

Diagram 316

1. •••   Bd3+   1. •••   Bd3+
2. Kg1   Rxe1+ 2. Re2   R/Bxe2

Diagram 317

1. •••   Rxe1+   1. •••   Rxe1+
2. Rxe1 Bd3+   2. Rxe1 Bd3+
3. Kg1   Rxe1+   3. Re2   B/Rxe2

Page 166

Diagram 318

1. Rd8+   Kxd8
2. Qxf7

Page 166

Diagram 319

1. Bxf7+   Qxf7
2. Rd8+   Kxd8
3. Qxf7

Page 167

Diagram 320

1. Qe7+   K moves
2. Qxf6

Diagram 321

1. Qe6+   Kg7
2. Qe7+   K moves
3. Qxf6

Page 168

Diagram 322

1. •••   Rh1+
2. Kxh1   Qxf2

Diagram 323

1. •••   Bc2+
2. Kxc2   Qxe4+

Page 169

Diagram 324

1. Rxh7+   Kxh7
2. Qxf6

Diagram 325

1. Rb7+ Kf8   1. Rb7+ Kh6/Kh8
2. Rxh7   2. Rxh7+ Kxh7
                3. Qxf6

Page 170

Diagram 326

1. •••   Nd4   1. •••   Nd4
2. Nxd4?? Qh2#   2. hxg4!   Nxe2+

Page 170

Diagram 327

1. •••   Bxc3   1. •••   Bxc3
2. bxc3   g5!   2. bxc3   g5!
3. N m.   Rxe2   3. B m.   gxf4

Page 171

Diagram 328

1. Nxe8   Rxe8
2. Qxf7

Diagram 329

1. Nxe5 Bxe5   1. Nxe5 Rfe8
2. Rxb4   2. Nf3

Page 172

Diagram 330

1. Rd8+   Bf8
2. Qxb2

Diagram 331

1. •••   Rxg6+
2. hxg6   Rxe4

Page 173

Diagram 332

1. Re8+ Rxe8   1. Re8+ Kg7
2. Qxd5   2. Rxd8

Diagram 333

1. Rf8+ Rxf8   1. Rf8+ Kh7
2. Qxe6   2. Qxe8

Page 174

Diagram 334

1. Rd8+ Kg7   1. Rd8+ Rxd8
2. Q/Rxc8   2. Qxc4

Diagram 335

1. Rd8+   Rxd8
2. Qxc4

Page 175

Diagram 336

1. ... Rb1+   1. ... Rb1+
2. Rxb1 Qxa3   2. Kf2?? Qe1#

Diagram 337

1. ... Rxd1+
2. Rxd1 Qxc3

Page 176

Diagram 338

1. Re8 Qxe8   1. Re8 Kf7
2. Qg7#   2. Qxf8#

Diagram 339

1. ... Re1+   1. ... Re1+
2. Nxe1 Qh1#   2. Qxe1 Qxg2#

Page 177

Diagram 340

1. Rxa6 Rxa6   1. Rxa6 Qxa6
2. Qd8#   2. Qd7#

Diagram 341

1. Rb8 Qxb8   1. Rb8 Rxb8
2. Nxf7#   2. Qg7#

Page 178

Diagram 342

Circle the Black Queen.

Page 179

Diagram 343

1. ... Qb3+
2. Ka1 Qa3+
3. Kb1 Qb3+, etc.
   draw

Page 179

Diagram 344

1. Qh5+ Kg8   1. Qe8+ Kh7
2. Qe8+ Kh7   2. Qh5+ Kg8
3. Qh5+, etc.   3. Qe8+, etc.
   draw   draw

Page 180

Diagram 345

1. Rxg6+ fxg6
2. Qxg6+ Kh8
3. Qh6+ Kg8
4. Qg6+, etc.
   draw

Diagram 346

1. Re8+ Rxe8
2. Qxe8+ Kh7
3. Qh5+ Kg8
4. Qe8+, etc.
   draw

Page 181

Diagram 347

1. ... Ng3+
2. Kh2 Nf1+
3. Kh1 Ng3+, etc.
   draw

Diagram 348

1. Ng6+ Kh7
2. Nf8+ Kh8
3. Ng6+, etc.
   draw

Page 182

Diagram 349

1. ... Na2+   1. ... Na2+
2. Kd1 Nc3+   2. Kb1 Nc3+
3. Kc1 Na2+, etc.   3. Ka1?? Ra2#
   draw

Page 182

Diagram 350

1. Nf6+ Kf8
2. Nd7+ Ke8/g8
3. Nf6+ Kf8
4. Nd7+, etc.
   draw

Page 183

Diagram 351

1. ... Ng4+   1. ... Ng4+
2. Kh1/h3 Nf2+   2. Kh1 Nf2+
3. Kh2 Ng4+   3. Kg1 Ng4+
4. Kh1/h3 Nf2+, etc.   4. Kh1 Nf2+
   draw   draw

Diagram 352

1. Nf5+ Kg8   1. Nf5+ Kh8??
2. Ne7/h6+ Kg7   2. g7+ Kg8
3. Nf5+ Kg8   3. Nh6#
4. Ne7/h6+ Kg7
   etc., draw

Page 184

Diagram 353

1. Bg6+ Kg8   1. Bf5/e4+? Qh6!
2. Bh7+ Kh8
3. Bg6+, etc.
   draw

Diagram 354

1. Be6+ Kh7
2. Bf5+ Kg8
3. Be6+, etc.
   draw

Page 185

Diagram 355

1. Rb7+ Ka8
2. Ra7+ Kb8
3. Rb7+, etc.
   draw

Page 185

Diagram 356

1. •••	Rg2+
2. Kh3	Rg3+
3. Kh2	Rg2+
4. Kh1	Rg1+, etc.
	draw

Page 186

Diagram 357

1. Rh7+	Kg8
2. Rhg7+	Kh8
3. Rh7+, etc.	
draw	

Diagram 358

1. Re8+	Ka7
2. Re7+	Ka8/b8
3. Re8+, etc.	
draw	

Page 187

Diagram 359

1. Rc8+	Ka7/b7
2. Rc7+	Ka8/b8
3. Rc8+, etc.	
draw	

Diagram 360

1. Qxb7+ Nxb7		1. Qxb7+ Nxb7	
2. Rxb7+ Ka8		2. Rxb7+ Kc8??	
3. Rxa7+ Kb8		3. Rhc7#	
4. Rab7+, etc.			
draw			

Page 188

Diagram 361

1. •••	Rxg3+
2. Kh1/h2	Rh3+
3. Kg1	Rg3+, etc.
	draw

Page 188

Diagram 362

1. •••	Qxg3+
2. hxg3	Rxg3+
3. Kh1/h2	Rh3+
4. Kg1	Rg3+, etc.
	draw

Page 189

Diagram 363

1. Qf8+	Kh7
2. Qf7+	Kh8
3. Qf8+, etc.	
draw	

Diagram 364

1. •••	Qg4+
2. Kh1	Qf3+
3. Kg1	Qg4+, etc.
	draw

Page 190

Diagram 365

1. Qe8+	Kh7
2. Qh5+	Kg8
3. Qe8+, etc.	
draw	

Diagram 366

1. Re8+	Rxe8
2. Qxe8+	Kh7
3. Qh5+	Kg8
4. Qe8+, etc.	
draw	

Page 191

Diagram 367

1. Qc7+	Kb5
2. Qb7+	Ka5
3. Qc7+, etc.	
draw	

Page 191

Diagram 368

1. Qg7/h8+	Ke7
2. Qf6+	Kf8
3. Qg7/h8+	Ke7
4. Qf6+, etc.	
draw	

Page 192

Diagram 369

1. Qg6+	Kh8
2. Qh6+	Kg8
3. Qg6+, etc.	
draw	

Diagram 370

1. Qxg6+	Kh8
2. Qxh6+	Kg8
3. Qg6+, etc.	
draw	

Page 193

Diagram 371

1. •••	Rxg3+
2. hxg3	Qxg3+
3. Kh1	Qh3+
4. Kg1	Qg3+, etc.
	draw

Diagram 372

1. •••	Rxb3+
2. a/cxb3	Rxb3+
3. a/cxb3	Qxb3+
4. Ka1	Qa3+, etc.
	draw

Page 194

Diagram 373

Circle the c8 square.

Page 195

Diagram 374

1. Kd6   Kf7/Kf8   1. Ra8/Rc8 Kf8
2. Rxd8/Rxd8+ 2. Rxd8+

Diagram 375

1. Rd3+ Qxd3   1. Rd3+ Kc4??
   stalemate 2. Rxg3

Page 196

Diagram 376

1. •••   Be3   1. •••   Be3
2. g4   Bf2#   2. N m.   Bg5#

Diagram 377

1. •••   Nc7+
2. Bxc7
   stalemate

Page 197

Diagram 378

1. Qf7   Kc8
2. Qc7/e8#

Diagram 379

1. h5   K moves
2. Bxf6

Page 198

Diagram 380

1. b4   Ka8   1. g8=Q/R??
2. g8=Q+ Ka7   stalemate
3. Qa2/b8#

Diagram 381

1. •••   g6   1. •••   g6
2. Ne3   Bf6# 2. Ne5   Bf2#

Page 199

Diagram 382

1. •••   Re3-e8
2. Kc1   Re1#

Page 199

Diagram 383

1. •••   Ra1-c1   1. •••   Ke3
2. Kg1   Rxe1+ 2. Kg1/Kg2 Rxe1

Page 200

Diagram 384

1. Rh8   Rxa7   1. Rh8   Kd6
2. Rh7+   K m.   2. a8=Q
3. Rxa7

Diagram 385

1. Rh8   Rxa7   1. Rh8   Kd6
2. Rh7+   K m.   2. a8=Q
3. Rxa7

Page 201

Diagram 386

1. Rh6   gxh6   1. Rh6   B m.
2. g7#   2. Rxh7#

Diagram 387

1. Rg5   Qxg5   1. Rg5   Qg6
2. hxg5   2. Rxg6

Page 202

Diagram 388

1. •••   Ng5
2. h7   Nf7#

Diagram 389

1. Nf7   g6   1. Kf7   g5
2. f/hxg6#   2. f/hxg6 e.p.#
               (en passant)

Page 203

Diagram 390

1. Rc4+ Qxc4   1. Rc4+ Kd5??
   stalemate 2. Rxc1

Page 203

Diagram 391

1. •••   Re6+   1. •••   Re6+
2. Qxe6   2. Kf5?? Rxb6
   stalemate

Page 204

Diagram 392

1. •••   Rf5+   1. •••   Rf5+
2. Kxf5   2. Ke4   Rxf3
   stalemate   3. Kxf3
                    draw

Diagram 393

1. •••   Rb6+   1. •••   Rb6+
2. Kxb6   2. Kc5   Rxd6
   stalemate   3. Kxd6
                    draw

Page 205

Diagram 394

1. •••   Rh5+
2. Kxh5
   stalemate

Diagram 395

1. •••   Rd6+   1. •••   Rd6+
2. K/Qxd6   2. K m.?? Rxf6
   stalemate

Page 206

Diagram 396

1. Bd4+ Bxd4   1. Bd4+ Kf7??
   stalemate 2. Bxb2

Diagram 397

1. Bd3+ Bxd3   1. Bd3+ Ka5/b6?
   stalemate 2. Bxe2

Page 207

Diagram 398

1. Qf2+ Qxf2   1. Qf2+ Kb8??
   stalemate 2. Qxf7

Page 207

Diagram 399

1.	•••	Qc7+	1.	•••	Qc7+
2.	Qxc7		2.	g3??	Qxd7
	stalemate				

Page 208

Diagram 400

1.	•••	Qxf4+	1.	•••	Qxf4+
2.	Qxf4		2.	Ke7??	Qxd2
	stalemate				

Diagram 401

| 1. | Qg8+ | Kxg8 |
| | | stalemate |

Page 209

Diagram 402

1. •••   Qh2+
2. Kxh2
    stalemate

Diagram 403

1.	•••	b1=Q+	1.	•••	b1=Q+
2.	Kh2	Qh1+	2.	Kh2	Qh1+
3.	Kxh1		3.	Kg3	Qxg2+
	stalemate		4.	Kxg2	
				stalemate	

Page 210

Diagram 404

1. Bd6++   K moves
2. Bxc5

Double Check
Discovered Check

Page 211

Diagram 405

1. Qg2+   K moves
2. Qxa8

Skewer

Page 211

Diagram 406

| 1. | Ke3 | Nf m. | 1. | Ke3 | Nd m. |
| 2. | Rxd8 | | 2. | Kxf3 | |

Discovered Attack

Page 212

Diagram 407

1. Qe4   R moves
2. Qxb7

Skewer

Diagram 408

1. c8=N+   K moves
2. Nxe7

Promoting a Pawn
(Underpromotion)

Page 213

Diagram 409

| 1. | d5+ | Qf6 | 1. | d5+ | Kg8?? |
| 2. | Bxf6+ | | 2. | dxe6 | |

Discovered Check

Diagram 410

1. Qa4   a6
2. c4   Any move
3. cxb5

Pin

Page 214

Diagram 411

| 1. | Bd6+ | K m. | 1. | Bd6+ | Ne7?? |
| 2. | Bxc5 | | 2. | Qxe7# | |

Discovered Check

Diagram 412

| 1. | Qf2+ | Qxf2 | 1. | Qf2+ | Kb8?? |
| | | stalemate | 2. | Qxf7 | |

Zugzwang/Stalemate

Page 215

Diagram 413

1. Rxe4   Rxe4
2. Bd3   Any move
3. Bxe4

Pin

Diagram 414

| 1. | Bg5++ | Ke8 | 1. | Bg5++ | Kc7 |
| 2. | Rd8# | | 2. | Bd8# | |

Double Check
Discovered Check

Page 216

Diagram 415

1. Rh7+   Nxh7
2. Rxh7+   K moves
3. Rxb7

Skewer

Diagram 416

| 1. | ••• | Ng4+ | 1. | ••• | Ng4+ |
| 2. | Bxg4 | Bxd4 | 2. | K m.? | Bxd4 |

Discovered Attack

Page 217

Diagram 417

1. Rxd8+   Rxd8
2. Qe8+   Rxe8
3. Rxe8#

Back Rank Combination

Diagram 418

1.	Qe4	Qh5	1.	Qe4	Re8??
2.	Qxe7		2.	Qxh7+	Kf8
			3.	Qh8#	

Double Threat

Page 218

Diagram 419

1. Rxb6+   K moves
2. Rxb7

Discovered Check

Diagram 420

1. Qxb6   axb6
2. a7   Any move
3. a8=Q

Promoting a Pawn

Page 219

Diagram 421

1. Ra8+   Kh7
2. Be4+   g6
3. Bxd3

Other Forks
(Bishop Fork)

Diagram 422

1. Re8+   Rxe8
2. Qxe8+   Kh7
3. Qh5+   Kg8
4. Qe8+, etc.
    draw

Perpetual Check

Page 220

Diagram 423

1. Rh6   gxh6   1. Rh6   B m.
2. g7#   2. Rxh7#

Zugzwang/Stalemate

Diagram 424

1. •••   Bd4+
2. Kh1   Rf1#

Back Rank Combination

Page 221

Diagram 425

1. Re7   g6   1. Re7   Qxe7??
2. Rxd7   2. Qxh7#

Double Threat

Diagram 426

1. Bxf7+   Kxf7
2. Qxg4

Discovered Attack

Page 222

Diagram 427

1. •••   Rxb3+
2. a/cxb3   Rxb3+
3. a/cxb3   Qxb3+
4. Ka1   Qa3+, etc.
       draw

Perpetual Check

Diagram 428

1. Rxh7+   Kxh7
2. Qxf6

Removing the Guard

Page 223

Diagram 429

1. R/Qb8+   Qxb8
2. R/Qxb8+   Re8
3. R/Qxe8#

Back Rank Combination

Diagram 430

1. •••   Qxf3
2. gxf3   Ne2+
3. K moves   Nxd4

Removing the Guard
Knight Fork

Page 224

Diagram 431

1. •••   Rg1+
2. Kxg1   Qxe2

Removing the Guard

Diagram 432

1. Rxh3   Rxh3
2. Bxe6+   K moves
3. Bxh3

Other Forks
(Bishop Fork)

Page 225

Diagram 433

1. •••   Qg1+
2. Kxg1   Nxe2+
3. K moves   Nxc1

Removing the Guard
Knight Fork

Diagram 434

1. Rxg7+   Kxg7
2. Qd4+   K moves
3. Qxa7

Other Forks
(Queen Fork)

Student Notes

On the following boards, record favorite opening positions, end positions, checkmating positions, and stalemating positions.

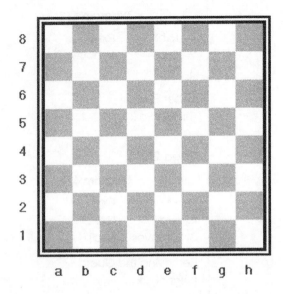

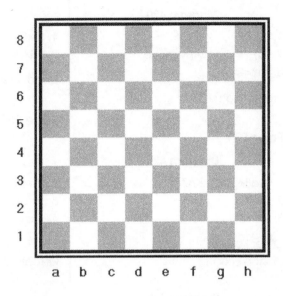

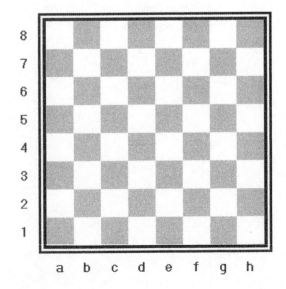

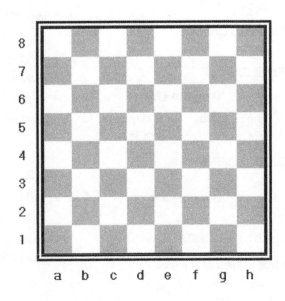

Student Notes

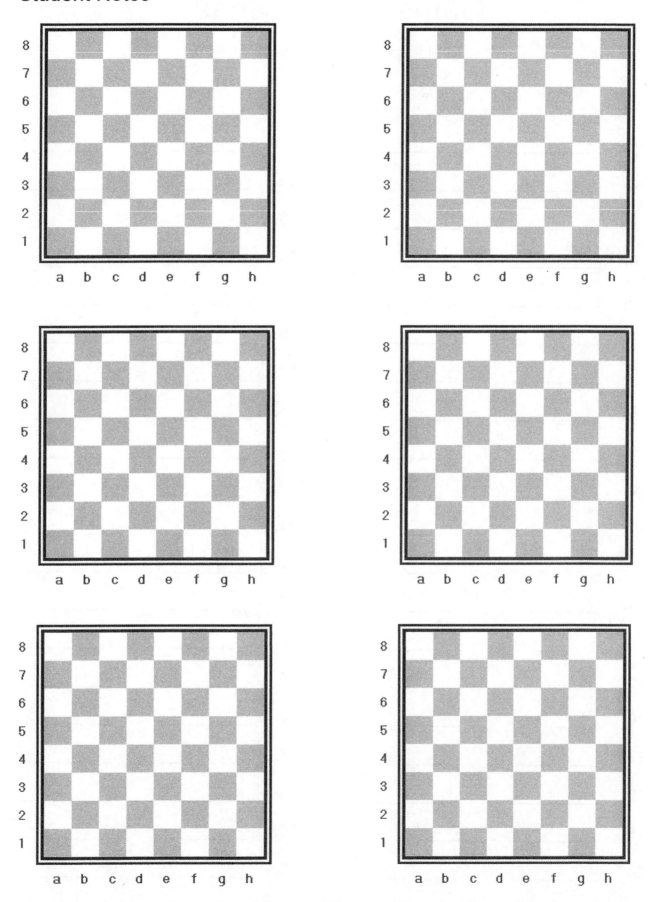

Game Record Sheet

Photocopy Master for Student Use

White	Black		White	Black
1. _____	_____	21. _____	_____
2. _____	_____	22. _____	_____
3. _____	_____	23. _____	_____
4. _____	_____	24. _____	_____
5. _____	_____	25. _____	_____
6. _____	_____	26. _____	_____
7. _____	_____	27. _____	_____
8. _____	_____	28. _____	_____
9. _____	_____	29. _____	_____
10. _____	_____	30. _____	_____
11. _____	_____	31. _____	_____
12. _____	_____	32. _____	_____
13. _____	_____	33. _____	_____
14. _____	_____	34. _____	_____
15. _____	_____	35. _____	_____
16. _____	_____	36. _____	_____
17. _____	_____	37. _____	_____
18. _____	_____	38. _____	_____
19. _____	_____	39. _____	_____
20. _____	_____	40. _____	_____

Game Record Sheet

	White	Black		White	Black
41.	_____	_____	61.	_____	_____
42.	_____	_____	62.	_____	_____
43.	_____	_____	63.	_____	_____
44.	_____	_____	64.	_____	_____
45.	_____	_____	65.	_____	_____
46.	_____	_____	66.	_____	_____
47.	_____	_____	67.	_____	_____
48.	_____	_____	68.	_____	_____
49.	_____	_____	69.	_____	_____
50.	_____	_____	70.	_____	_____
51.	_____	_____	71.	_____	_____
52.	_____	_____	72.	_____	_____
53.	_____	_____	73.	_____	_____
54.	_____	_____	74.	_____	_____
55.	_____	_____	75.	_____	_____
56.	_____	_____	76.	_____	_____
57.	_____	_____	77.	_____	_____
58.	_____	_____	78.	_____	_____
59.	_____	_____	79.	_____	_____
60.	_____	_____	80.	_____	_____

Other Chess Books by John A. Bain

Chess Rules for Students

Chess Rules For Students is an instructional workbook designed for students just learning the game of chess. Parents and coaches unfamiliar with chess will find this booklet a valuable beginner's guide.

- No previous chess experience needed.

- Reading level is appropriate for grade-school use.

- All major rules of chess are covered.

- Pages are in easy-to-use worksheet format.

- Page-by-page comprehensive activities assess student understanding.

- Student-friendly Answer Key makes self-correction fun.

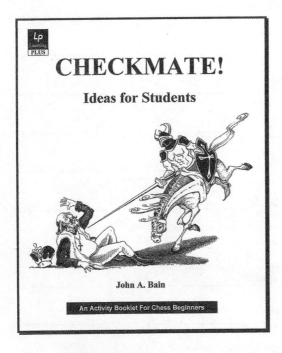

Checkmate! Ideas for Students

Checkmate! Ideas for Students is an instructional workbook for students who have mastered basic chess rules, beginning chess play, and the use of chess notation.

- Reading level is appropriate for grade-school use.

- Pages are in easy-to-use worksheet format.

- Page-by-page activities allow teachers to assess student understanding and progress.

- Activities are comprehensive, yet easy to correct.

- Versatile format enables both independent study and group instruction.

- Student-friendly Answer Key makes self-correction fun.

Each of these books is available from your favorite chess materials distributor, or you may contact the publisher directly by mail at the address given on the back cover. On the web, visit **www.chessforstudents.com**.